Speed Math – Quick and Easy Calculations

Anjum Pasha

Contents

SYNOPSIS

Speed Math or Vedic Math dates back to the Vedic times when all calculations were done mentally. To improve the efficiency of calculations Vedic techniques were developed, learned, and practiced. These techniques were continuously used till recent days when calculators and computers started replacing the mental calculations. Calculators and computers have been effective tools for any calculation however; they handicap the user by decreasing his utilization of mind. Excessive dependence on calculators and computers not only affect the mathematical skills but also the general aptitude of people.

By using speed math the audiences not only learn techniques to solve math problems with great speed but also enhance their thinking and analyzing skills in various fields. With continuous use of these methods one can see definite change in their approach towards everyday activities.

This book can be used by all audiences ranging from students, to teachers, to parents, and to adults for varied purposes. Students who dislike the conventional ways of solving math problems can use these techniques to create a liking towards the subject. They can always perform quick checks to see if they have done the math correctly in their answers. Competitive exam aspirants can use these techniques to solve the math problems quickly which is the key to score in these exams.

This book has been written in a simple manner to be easily understood by audiences of any age group.

This book contains 8 chapters with each chapter focusing on one mathematical operation. Each chapter begins with a detailed introduction to the concepts that will be required for that operation. Next, examples are presented to cover almost all possible types of problems for the respective math operation. Every example follows the two steps approach. In the first step the problem is presented with a quick solution where the learner can appreciate the effectiveness of the technique in a single step. Next the same problem is presented in detailed steps where the learner can learn the quick solution details. At the end of each section exercises are provided to reinforce the learning. Answers to these exercises are provided at the end of the book.

Chapter 1. QUICK AND EASY MULTIPLICATION

BASES AND COMPLEMENTS

What are Bases and Complements?

- Introduction to Bases

  Bases are numbers starting with 1 and followed by 0s.
  The following are examples of bases 10, 10000, 100,
  100000000 and the following are examples of not bases 101,
  1100, 200, 546, 100000001

- Introduction to complements
  - Complements are the two numbers which when added results in
    the next base.
    In the example $6 + 4 = 10$, 6 and 4 are complements since, 6 and 4
    when added give the next base 10.
    In the example $456 + 544 = 1000$, 456 and 544 are complements
    since, 456 and 544 when added give the next base 1000
  - To find the complement of any number perform "*All from 9 and
    last from 10*" – subtract all digits from 9 and the last digit from 10

(1) Find the complement of 3592

- Quick solution: Complement of 3592 is 6408

ailed steps: Perform "*All from 9 and last from 10*" for the number 592

$$(9-3)(9-5)(9-9)(10-2) \xrightarrow{Results\ in} 6408$$

Therefore, the complement of 3592 is 6408

(2) Find the complement of 786540

- Quick solution: Complement of 786540 is 213460

- Detailed steps: Perform "*All from 9 and last from 10*" for the number 786540

$$(9-7)(9-8)(9-6)(9-5)(10-4)$$

$$\left(\xrightarrow{Last\ digit} 0\ retain\ as\ is \right) \qquad \xrightarrow{Results\ in} 213460$$

Therefore, the complement of 786540 is 213460

Exercise 1- Find the complement of

1. 47348	2. 36590	3. 3557	4. 2070
5. 98989	6. 99990	7. 11000	8. 2748

MENTAL MULTIPLICATION WITH 9s

Rules for multiplying with 9s

- For multiplication with 9s, consider 9s as the multiplier and the other number as the multiplicand. In the example $654 * 999$, 654 is the multiplicand and 999 is the multiplier.

- Use this technique if the number of digits in the multiplicand is less than or equal to the number of digits in the multiplier (9s) or if the digits in the multiplicand is greater than the digits in the multiplier (9s)

  o If the number of digits in the multiplicand is less than the number of digits in the multiplier (for example, 64 * 9999) make the number of digits equal by adding 0s in front of the multiplicand.

  o If the number of digits in the multiplicand is greater than the number of digits in the multiplier, split the multiplicand into the LHS part and the RHS part. The number of digits in the RHS part should be equal to the number of digits in the multiplier. In the example 3974284 * 999, split the multiplicand 3974284 into two parts. The LHS part should be 3974 and the RHS part should be 284. The number of digits in the RHS part (3 digits) should equal the number of digits in the multiplier (999).

(1) Perform 24 * 999

- Quick solution: 24 * 999 $\xrightarrow[\substack{RHS\ part\ of\ answer \\ Complement\ of\ 024}]{\substack{LHS\ part\ of\ answer \\ Decrement\ multiplicand\ 24}}$ 23
  976

  Therefore, 24 * 999 = 23976

- Detailed Steps: Note that the multiplicand 24 has less number of digits (2 digits) than the number of digits in the multiplier 999 (3 digits).

  Step 1. Make the number of digits in the multiplier 24 equal to the number of digits in the multiplicand

  24 $\xrightarrow{Translates\ to}$ 024

Step 2.   Find the LHS of the answer

Decrement 024 by 1

$024 - 1 = 023$

Therefore, 023 is the LHS part of the answer.

Step 3.   Find the RHS of the answer

Find the compliment of 024

$024 \xrightarrow{\text{Compliment of } 024} 976$

Therefore, 976 is the RHS part of the answer

Step 4.   Combine the LHS part and the RHS part for the final

answer

Therefore, $24 * 999 = 23976$

(2) Perform $462 * 99$

- Quick solution: $462 * 99$

$\xrightarrow{\text{1st part } 462} 4$

$\xrightarrow{\text{2nd part } 462} 62$

$4 \xrightarrow{\text{LHS part of answer}} 4 + 1 = 5; 462 - 5 = 457$

$62 \xrightarrow[\text{Complement of } 62]{\text{RHS part of answer}} 38$

Therefore, $462 * 99 = 45738$

- Detailed Steps: Note that the multiplier 99 has less digits (2 digits) when compared to multiplicand 462 which has 3 digits

Step 1.   Split the multiplicand 462 into the 1st part and the 2nd part

Note that the number of digits in the 2nd part should be equal to the number of digits in the multiplier 99.

$$462 \xrightarrow{Split\ into} 4\ and\ 62$$

Step 2.   Find the LHS part of the answer

2.1.   Increment the 1st part of 462 by 1

$$4 + 1 = 5$$

2.2.   Subtract 5 from multiplicand 462

$$462 - 5 = 457$$

Therefore, 457 is the LHS part of the answer

Step 3.   Find the RHS part of the answer

Find the compliment of 2nd part of 462

$$62 \xrightarrow{Compliment\ of\ 62} 38$$

Therefore, 38 is the RHS part of the answer

Step 4.   Combine the LHS part and the RHS part for the answer

Therefore, $462 * 99 = 45738$

Exercise 2- Solve mental multiplication with 9s problems

1. **3081 * 9**	2. **7826 * 99**	3. **8703 * 999**
4. **8393 * 9999**	5. 5777 * 9999	6. 5429 * 99
7. **72713 * 9**	8. 6071 * 99	9. 5576 * 999
10. **1769 * 9**	11. 81339 * 999	12. 89306 * 999
13. **60 * 9999**	14. 631 * 99	15. 4392 * 999
16. **4927 * 9**		

MULTIPLICATION WITH 1s

Rules for multiplying with 1s

- For these exercises always consider 1s as the multiplier and the other number as the multiplicand. In the example $654 * 111$, 654 is the multiplicand and 111 is the multiplier

- If the multiplier is 2 digits (11) add one @ $(2 - 1 = 1)$ symbol at the beginning and at the end of the multiplicand. Note that these @ symbols are 0s that are only used for calculation purpose and do not posses any actual value by themselves. If the multiplier is 3 digits (111) add 2@ symbols $(3 - 1 = 2)$ at the beginning and at the end of the multiplicand.

- If the multiplier is 2 digits (11) perform successive addition of 2 consecutive digits in the multiplicand. If the multiplier is 3 digits (111) perform successive addition of 3 consecutive digits in the multiplicand and so on

(1) Perform $732 * 111$

- Quick solution:

$$732 \xrightarrow{\textit{Introduce symbols}} @@732@@ \xrightarrow{\textit{Results in}} 7 \ 10 \ 12 \ 5 \ 2$$

$$\xrightarrow{\textit{Solution is}} 8 \ 1 \ 2 \ 5 \ 2$$

Therefore, $732 * 111 = 81252$

- Detailed Steps:

Step 1.   Add the redundant @ symbols to the multiplicand 732

Since the multiplier (111) is a 3 digit number add 3-1 = 2 @

symbols on the left end and 2 @ symbols on the right end of the multiplier 732. Note that these @ symbols represent 0s for calculation purpose only without changing the multiplier value.

Therefore, $732 \xrightarrow{\textit{Introducing symbols}} {}_{@@}732_{@@}$

Step 2.   Add successive digits in the multiplicand starting from the RHS

As the multiplier 111 is a 3 digit number, begin by adding 3 successive digits in the multiplicand $_{@@}732_{@@}$ each time from the RHS to the LHS

2.1.   Add first 3 digits in $_{@@}732_{@@}$ from the RHS to get the answer digits $_{@@}73\textbf{2}_{@@} \xrightarrow{\textit{Add first 3 digits from RHS}}$

$2 + 0 + 0 = 2$

Therefore, 2 forms the first digit in the answer

2.2.   Add the next 3 digits in $_{@@}732_{@@}$ to get the next answer digit $_{@@}7\textbf{32}_{@@} \xrightarrow{\textit{Add next 3 digits from RHS}}$

$3 + 2 + 0 = 5$

Therefore, 5 forms the next digit in the answer

2.3.   Add the next 3 digits to get the next answer digit

$_{@@}\textbf{732}_{@@} \xrightarrow{\textit{Add next 3 digits from RHS}}$

$7 + 3 + 2 = 12$

Therefore, 2 forms the next digit in the answer and 1 is carried to the next step

2.4.   Add the next 3 digits in $_{@@}732_{@@}$ and the 1 carried from the previous step to get the next answer digit

$_{@@}\textbf{73}2_{@@} \xrightarrow{\substack{\textit{Add next 3 digits} \\ \textit{and 1 carried forward}}}$

$(0 + 7 + 3) + 1 = 11$

Therefore, 1 forms the next digit in the answer and 1 is carried to the next step

2.5. Add the next 3 digits in $@@732@@$ and the 1 carried from the previous step

$$@@732@@ \xrightarrow{\substack{Add\ next\ 3\ digits \\ and\ 1\ carried\ forward}}$$

$(0 + 0 + 7) + 1 = 8$

Therefore, 8 forms the next digit in the answer and 1 is carried to the next step

Step 3.   Combine all the digits in the answer for the final solution

Therefore, $732 * 111 = 81252$

(2) Perform 2453 * 11

- Quick solution:

$$2453 \xrightarrow{Introducing\ symbols} @2453@ \xrightarrow{Results\ in} 2\,6\,9\,8\,3$$

Therefore, $2453 * 11 = 26983$

- Detailed Steps:

Step 1.   Add the redundant @ to the multiplicand 2453

Since the multiplier (11) is a 2 digit number add 2-1 = 1 @ symbol on the left end and 1 @ symbol on the right end of the multiplier 2453.

Therefore, $2453 \xrightarrow{Transforms\ to} @2453@$

Step 2.   Add the successive digits in the multiplicand 2453 starting from the RHS.

As the multiplier 11 is a 2 digit number, begin by adding 2 digits in the multiplicand (2453) each time starting from the RHS to the LHS

2.1. Add the first 2 digits in 2453 from the RHS to get the answer digits $@2453_@$ $\xrightarrow{Add\ first\ 2\ digits\ from\ RHS}$ $3 + 0 = 3$

Therefore, 3 forms the first digit in the answer

2.2. Add the next 2 digits in 2453 to get the next answer digit

$@2453_@$ $\xrightarrow{Add\ next\ 2\ digits\ from\ RHS}$ $5 + 3 = 8$

Therefore, 8 forms the next digit in the answer

2.3. Add the next 2 digits to get the next answer digit

$@2453_@$ $\xrightarrow{Add\ next\ 2\ digits\ from\ RHS}$ $4 + 5 = 9$

Therefore, 9 forms the next digit in the answer

Step 3.   Add the rest of the successive two digits and combine all the digits in the answer for the final solution

Therefore, $2453 * 11 = 26983$

Exercise 3- Solve multiplication with 1s problems

1. 45293 * 11	2. 57075 * 111	3. 80106 * 11	4. 792 * 11
5. 94644 * 111	6. 5518 * 1111	7. 482 * 1111	8. 6686 * 1111
9. 4903 * 11111	10. 898 * 1111	11. 4071 * 1111	12. 44 * 1111
13. 55739 * 111	14. 395 * 1111	15. 3231 * 11111	16. 52 * 1111

MULTIPLICATION WITH MULTIPLES OF 11

Rules for multiplication with 12, 13 and so on

- For these exercises consider 12, 13, 14… as the multiplier and the other number as the multiplicand. In the example $654 * 15$, 654 is the multiplicand and 15 is the multiplier

- If the multiplier is 12, multiply the first digit in the multiplicand by 2 and add it to the previous digit. If the multiplier is 13, multiply the first digit in the multiplicand by 3 and add it to the previous digit and so on

(1) Perform $731 * 12$

- Quick solution: $731 \xrightarrow{Transforms\ to} @731@$

$\xrightarrow{Results\ in} (2 * 0 + 7)(2 * 7 + 3)(2 * 3 + 1)(2 * 1 + 0)$

$\xrightarrow{Results\ in} 7\ 17\ 7\ 2 \xrightarrow{Results\ in} 8\ 7\ 7\ 2$

Therefore, $731 * 12 = 8772$

- Detailed Steps:

Step 1.   Since the multiplier (12) is a 2 digit number add 2-1 = 1 @ symbol at the beginning and 1 @ symbol at the end of the multiplicand 731.

Therefore, $731 \xrightarrow{Transforms\ to} @731@$

Step 2.   Begin with the RHS, considering two successive digits multiply the first number with 2 (since the multiplier is 12) and add the next number to the product

2.1. Considering the first 2 digits in 731 from the RHS. Multiply the first number with 2 and add the product to the next digit

$$@731_@ * 12 \xrightarrow{\textit{Considering 1 and @}} (2 * 1) + 0 = 2$$

Therefore, 2 forms the first digit in the answer

2.2. Considering the next 2 digits in 731 from the RHS. Multiply the first number with 2 and add the product to the next digit

$$@731_@ * 12 \xrightarrow{\textit{considering 3 and 1}} (2 * 3) + 1 = 7$$

Therefore, 7 forms the next digit in the answer

2.3. Considering the next 2 digits in 731. Multiply the first number with 2 and add the product to the next digit

$$@731_@ * 12 \xrightarrow{\textit{considering 7 and 3}} (2 * 7) + 3 = 17$$

Therefore, 7 forms the next digit in the answer and 1 is carried over to next step

2.4. Considering the next 2 digits perform

$$@731_@ * 12 \xrightarrow[\textit{adding 1 carried forward}]{\textit{Considering @ and 7 and}} (2 * 0) + 7 + 1 = 8$$

Therefore, 8 forms the next digit in the answer

Step 3. Combine all the digits in the answer for the final solution

Therefore, $731 * 12 = 8772$

(2) Perform 321 * 14

- Quick solution: $321 \xrightarrow{\textit{Transforms to}} @321_@$

$$\xrightarrow{\textit{Results in}} (4 * 0 + 3)(4 * 3 + 2)(4 * 2 + 1)(4 * 1 + 0)$$

$$\xrightarrow{\textit{Results in}} 3\ 14\ 9\ 4 \xrightarrow{\textit{Results in}} 4\ 4\ 9\ 4$$

Therefore, $321 * 14 = 4494$

- Detailed Steps:

Step 1.   Since the multiplier (14) is a 2 digit number add 2-1 = 1 @ symbol at the beginning and 1 @ symbol at the end of the multiplicand 321.

Therefore, $321 \xrightarrow{Transforms\ to} @321@$

Step 2.   Begin with the RHS, considering two successive digits multiply the first number with 4 (since the multiplier is 14) and add the product to the next digit

2.1.   Considering the first 2 digits in 321 from the RHS. Multiply the first number with 4 and add the product to the next digit

$@321@ \xrightarrow{Considering\ 1\ and\ @} (4*1) + 0 = 4$

Therefore, 4 forms the first digit in the answer

2.2.   Considering the next 2 digits in 321 from the RHS. Multiply the first number with 4 and add the product to the next digit

$@321@ \xrightarrow{Considering\ 2\ and\ 1} (4*2) + 1 = 9$

Therefore, 9 forms the next digit in the answer

2.3.   Considering the next 2 digits

$@321@ \xrightarrow{Considering\ 3\ and\ 2} (4*3) + 2 = 14$

Therefore, 4 forms the next digit in the answer and 1 is carried over to next step

2.4.   Considering the next 2 digits and 1 brought forward from the previous step perform

$@321@ \xrightarrow{Considering\ @\ and\ 3} (4*0) + 3 + 1 = 4$

Therefore, 4 forms the next digit in the answer

Step 3.   Combine all the digits in the answer for the final solution

Therefore, $321 * 14 = 4494$

Exercise 4- Solve multiplication with multiples of 11 problems

1. 7606 *	2. 90723 *	3. 72770 *	4. 37401 *
12	14	13	12
5. 1701 *	6. 6836 *	7. 9039 *	8. 8444 *
14	12	14	13
9. 503 * 13	10. 8448 *	11. 5506 *	12. 2794 *
	15	12	14

MULTIPLICATION OF NUMBERS CLOSE TO BASES

Rules for multiplying numbers close to bases

1. Numbers close to the base can be less than their respective bases (97, 98, 989) or greater than their respective bases (1011, 102, 12)

2. Derive the answer in two parts, the LHS part and the RHS part

3. Number of digits in the RHS part of the answer should be equal to the number of 0s in the base

(1) Perform 94 * 93

- Quick solution:

$$\xrightarrow{LHS\ part\ of\ the\ answer} \begin{matrix} 94 & -6 \\ 93 & -7 \end{matrix} \xrightarrow{Implies} 93 - 6\ or\ 94 - 7 = 87$$

$$\xrightarrow{RHS\ part\ of\ the\ answer} (-6) * (-7) = 42$$

Therefore, 94 * 93 = 8742

- Detailed Steps: Both the multiplicand and the multiplier are less than its base 100

Step 1.   Find the difference of the multiplier and the multiplicand numbers from its base

$$94 - 100 = -6$$

$$93 - 100 = -7$$

Step 2.   Find the LHS part of the answer

Perform cross addition of the numbers and the differences

$$94 - 100 = -6$$

$$93 - 100 = -7$$

$\xrightarrow{\textit{Cross addition}}$ $94 + (-7) = 87 \text{ or } 93 + (-6) = 87$

Therefore, 87 is the LHS part of the answer

Step 3.   Find the RHS part of the answer

$$94 - 100 = -6$$

3.1.   Multiply the differences to get the RHS

$$93 - 100 = -7$$

$\xrightarrow{\textit{Multiplication of differences}}$ $(-6) * (-7) = 42$

3.2.   Make the number of digits in the RHS part of the answer equal to the number of 0s in the base 100. In this case the number of digits in 42 (2 digits) equals the number of 0s in 100 (2 0s).

Therefore, 42 is the RHS part of the answer.

Step 4.   Combine the LHS part and the RHS part of the answer to get the final solution.

Therefore, $94 * 93 = 8742$

(2) Perform $86 * 87$

- Quick solution:

$$\xrightarrow{\text{LHS part of the answer}}$$

$$86 \quad -14$$

$$\xrightarrow{\text{Implies}} 87 - 14 \; or \; 86 - 13 = 73$$

$$87 \quad -13$$

$$\xrightarrow{\text{RHS part of the answer}} (-14) * (-13) = 182$$

$$\xrightarrow[\text{Implies}]{\text{Retain 2 digits in RHS part}} 82$$

$$\xrightarrow{\text{1 carried over from RHS to LHS}} 73 + 1 = 74$$

Therefore, $86 * 87 = 7482$

- Detailed Steps: Both the multiplicand and multiplier are less than its base 100

Step 1.   Find the difference of the multiplier and multiplicand numbers from its base

$$86 - 100 = -14$$

$$87 - 100 = -13$$

Step 2.   Find the LHS part of the answer

Perform cross addition of the numbers and the differences

$$86 - 100 = -14$$

$$87 - 100 = -13$$

$$\xrightarrow{\text{Cross addition}} 86 + (-13) = 87 + (-14) = 73$$

Therefore, 73 is the LHS part of the answer

Step 3.   Find the RHS part of the answer

3.1.   Multiply the differences to get the RHS

$$86 - 100 = -14$$

$$87 - 100 = -13$$

$$\xrightarrow{\textit{Multiplication of differences}} (-14) * (-13) = 182$$

3.2. Make the number of digits in the RHS part of the answer equal to the number of 0s in the base 100. In this case the number of digits in 182 (3 digits) is more than the number of 0s in 100 (2 0s). Retain 82 (2 digits equal to 2 0s in 100) in the RHS part of the answer and carryover 1 to the LHS part of the answer.

The RHS part of the answer is 82.

Step 4.   Update the LHS part of the answer

Add the 1 carried over from the RHS part to the LHS part of the answer.

The LHS part of the answer becomes $73 + 1 = 74$

Step 5.   Combine the LHS part and the RHS part of the answer to get the final solution.

Therefore, $86 * 87 = 7482$

(3) Perform $9992 * 9890$

- Quick solution:

$$\xrightarrow{\textit{LHS part of the answer}}$$

$9992 \quad -8$

$$\xrightarrow{\textit{Implies}} 9890 - 8 \ or \ 9992 - 110 \ = 9882$$

$9890 \quad -110$

$$\xrightarrow{\textit{RHS part of the answer}} (-110) * (-8) = 0880$$

Therefore, $9992 * 9890 = 98820880$

- Detailed Steps: Both the multiplicand and multiplier are less than its base 10000

Step 1.   Find the difference of the multiplier and the multiplicand numbers from its base

$$9992 - 10000 = -8$$

$$9890 - 10000 = -110$$

Step 2.   Find the LHS part of the answer

Perform cross addition of the numbers with their differences

$$9992 - 10000 = -8$$

$$9890 - 10000 = -110$$

$\xrightarrow{Cross\ addition} 9992 - 110 = 9890 - 8 = 9882$

Therefore, 9882 is the LHS part of the answer

Step 3.   Find the RHS part of the answer

3.1.   Multiply the differences to get the RHS

$$9992 - 10000 = -8$$

$$9890 - 10000 = -110$$

$\xrightarrow{Multiplication\ of\ differences} (-8) * (-110) = 880$

3.2.   Make the number of digits in the RHS part of the answer equal to the number of 0s in the base 10000. In this case the number of digits in 880 (3 digits) are less than the number of 0s in 10000 (4 0s). Add 0 before 880 to make the number of digits equal.

Therefore, 0880 is the RHS part of the answer.

Step 4.   Combine the LHS part and the RHS part of the answer to get the final solution.

Therefore, $9992 * 9890 = 98820880$

(4) Perform $997 * 1008$

- Quick solution:

$\xrightarrow{LHS\ part\ of\ the\ answer}$

$997 \quad -3$

$\xrightarrow[\text{Implies}]{} 1008 - 3 \ or \ 997 + 8 = 1005$

$1008 \quad 8$

$\xrightarrow{RHS\ part\ of\ the\ answer} (-3) * (8) = -24 \xrightarrow{transforms\ to} -024$

$\xrightarrow[\substack{to\ remove\ negative\ sign}]{Borrow\ 1\ from\ LHS\ part\ to\ RHS\ part} 1000 - 024 = 976$

$\xrightarrow{LHS\ part\ of\ the\ answer\ becomes} 1005 - 1 = 1004$

Therefore, $997 * 1008 = 1004976$

- Detailed Steps: In this case one number (997) is below the base 1000 and the second number (1008) is above the base 1000. Note that the bases for both the numbers are the same which is 1000.

Step 1.   Find the difference of the numbers from its base

$997 - 1000 = -3$

$1008 - 1000 = 8$

Step 2.   Find the LHS part of the answer

Perform cross addition of the numbers and the differences

$997 - 1000 = -3$

$1008 - 1000 = 8$

$$\xrightarrow{Cross\ addition} 997 + 8 = 1008 - 3 = 1005$$

Therefore, 1005 is the LHS part of the answer

Step 3.   Find the RHS part of the answer

    3.1. Multiply the differences to get the RHS

$$997 - 1000 = -3$$

$$1008 - 1000 = 8$$

$$\xrightarrow{Multiplication\ of\ differences} (-3) * (8) = -24$$

    3.2. Make the number of digits in the RHS part of the answer equal to the number of 0s in the base 1000. In this case the number of digits in -24 (2 digits) are less than the number of 0s in 1000 (3 0s). Add 0 before -24 to make the number of digits equal.

        Therefore, -024 is the RHS part of the answer.

    3.3. Remove the negative sign from the RHS part of the answer

        Borrow 1 from the LHS part of the answer and perform the operation $1000 - 024 = 976$

        Therefore, 976 forms the RHS part of the answer.

        Note that borrowing 1 from the LHS part is equal to borrowing 1000

Step 4.   Update the LHS part of the answer

Decrement 1 from the LHS part as it was carried forward to the RHS part in the previous step.

Therefore, the LHS part of the answer is $1005 - 1 = 1004$

Step 5.   Combine the LHS part and the RHS part of the answer to get the final solution.

Therefore, $997 * 1008 = 1004976$

(5) Perform $103 * 1005$

- Quick solution:

$$103 * 1005 \xrightarrow{transforms\ to} 1030 * 1005$$

$$\xrightarrow{LHS\ part\ of\ the\ answer} \begin{array}{cc} 1030 & 30 \\ \\ 1005 & 5 \end{array} \xrightarrow{Implies} 1005 + 30 = 1035$$

$$\xrightarrow{RHS\ part\ of\ the\ answer} (30) * \frac{(5)}{\underset{\longrightarrow 10}{Ratio\ of\ bases}} = 15$$

Therefore, $103 * 1005 = 103515$

- Detailed Steps: In this case both the numbers have different bases. The number 103 has a base of 100 while the number 1005 has a base of 1000 and also both the numbers are above their respective bases.

Step 1.   Bring both the number to the same base

1.1. Find the ratio of the two bases.

Therefore, $\frac{1000}{100} = 10$ is the ratio

1.2. Multiply the smaller number 103 with the ratio to make the bases equal. At the last step divide the answer with this ratio to compensate for this multiplication

Therefore, the new multiplicand is $103 * 10 = 1030$

Now both the numbers (1030 and 1005) belong to the same base 1000

Step 2.   Find the difference of the numbers from its base

$1030 - 1000 = 30$

$1005 - 1000 = 5$

Step 3.   Find the LHS part of the answer

Perform cross addition of the numbers and the differences

$1030 - 1000 = 30$

$1005 - 1000 = 5$

$\xrightarrow{Cross\ addition} 1030 + 5 = 1005 + 30 = 1035$

Therefore, 1035 forms the LHS part of the answer

Step 4.   Find the RHS part of the answer

4.1. Multiply the differences to get the RHS

$1030 - 1000 = 30$

$1005 - 1000 = 5$

$\xrightarrow{Multiplication\ of\ differences} (30) * (5) = 150$

4.2. Make the number of digits in the RHS part of the answer equal to the number of 0s in the base 1000. In this case the number of digits in 150 (3 digits) are equal to the number of 0s in base 1000 (3 0s).

Therefore, 150 forms the RHS part of the answer.

4.3. Compensate for the multiplication with the ratio done in step 2 by dividing the RHS part by the ratio

Therefore, the RHS part of the answer is $\frac{150}{10} = 15$

Step 5.   Combine the LHS part and the RHS part of the answer for the final solution

Therefore, $103 * 1005 = 103515$

(6) Perform $503 * 508$

- Quick solution:

  LHS part of the answer
  $\longrightarrow$

  503   3
  $\xrightarrow{Implies} 508 + 3 \; or \; 503 + 8 = 511$
  508   8

  $\xrightarrow{LHS \; valu* \; ratio \; of \; 500/100} 511 * 5 = 2555$

  $\xrightarrow{RHS \; part \; of \; the \; answer} 8 * 3 = 24$

  Therefore, $503 * 508 = 255524$

- Detailed Steps: As these numbers are not close to any of the base 100 or to the base 1000, consider any closer base (100) as the real base. Also, as these numbers are close to 500, consider 500 as the working base. While solving problems like these ensure that the working base in greater than the real base.

Step 1.   Find the difference of the numbers from its working base

$$503 - 500 = 3$$

$$508 - 500 = 8$$

Step 2.   Find the LHS part of the answer

2.1. Perform cross addition of the numbers and the differences

$$503 - 500 = 3$$

$$508 - 500 = 8$$

$\xrightarrow{Cross \; addition} 503 + 8 = 508 + 3 = 511$

Therefore, 511 is the arrived LHS part

2.2. Compensate for having used the working base (500) instead of real base (100)

Find the ratio of working base to real base

$$\frac{WB\ 500}{RB\ 100} = 5$$

Multiply the ratio with the LHS to arrive at the final LHS part of the answer $5 * 511 = 2555$

Therefore, the LHS part of the answer is 2555

Step 3.   Find the RHS part of the answer

   3.1.   Multiply the differences to get the RHS

        $503 - 500 = 3$

        $508 - 500 = 8$

$$\xrightarrow{Multiplication\ of\ differences} (3) * (8) = 24$$

   3.2.   Make the number of digits in the RHS part of the answer equal to the number of 0s in the base 100. In this case the number of digits in 24 (2 digits) are equal to the number of 0s in base 100 (2 0s).

Therefore, 24 form the RHS part of the answer.

Step 4.   Combine the LHS part and the RHS part of the answer for the final solution

Therefore, $503 * 508 = 255524$

Exercise 5- Solve multiplication with numbers close to bases

1. **87 * 95**	2. **83 *** **93**	3. **83 *** **90**	4. **80 *** **103**
5. **85 * 106**	6. **89 *** **107**	7. **103 *** **93**	8. **105 *** **94**
9. **103 * 498**	10. **994 *** **94**	11. **102 *** **105**	12. **103 *** **102**

ANY NUMBER MULTIPLICATION

Rules for multiplying any number

- Make the number of digits in the multiplicand and the multiplier equal by adding 0s at the beginning of any number
- Write the pattern based on the number of digits in the multiplicand and the multiplier.
    - For 2 x 2 multiplication remember the pattern 1,2,1 where the comma separates the digits in the answer. For example to multiply any number a2a1 with b2b1 perform the following

      $(a2 * b2), (a2 * b1 + a1 * b2), (a1 * b1)$.
    - For 3 x 3 multiplication, remember the pattern 1,2, 3, 2, 1 where the comma separates the digits in the answer.
    - For example to multiply any number a3a2a1 with b3b2b1 perform the following

      $(a3 * b3), (a3 * b2 + a2 * b3), (a3 * b1 + a2 * b2 + a1 * b3),$
      $(a2 * b1 + a1 * b2), (a1 * b1)$.
    - Similarly the pattern for higher digits
- Find the digits in the answer based on the pattern

(1) Perform $493 * 162$

- Quick solution:

      493 *Cross multiplication and Addition* →

      162

      $(4 * 1)(4 * 6 + 9 * 1)(4 * 2 + 9 * 6 + 3 * 1)(9 * 2 + 3 * 6)(6)$

$\xrightarrow{\text{Results in}} (4)(33)(65)(36)(6) \xrightarrow{\text{Results in}} 7\,9\,8\,6\,6$

Therefore, $493 * 162 = 79866$

- Detailed Steps: Since this is a 3 x 3 multiplication use the sequence 12321, where the sequence will be the digits in the answer

Step 1.   Start the multiplication of digits from the RHS by referring to the first sequence number 12321. The number 1 implies that only 1 digit from each multiplicand and multiplier has to be multiplied.

4 9 3

$\xrightarrow{\text{Multiplication of 3 and 2}} 3 * 2 = 6$

1 6 2

Therefore, $493 * 162 = $ _____ 6

Step 2.   Perform the next cross multiplication and addition referring to the sequence 12321. The number 2 implies that two digits each from multiplicand and multiplier have to be

multiplied.   4 9 3

$\xrightarrow[\text{Addition}]{\substack{\text{Cross multiplication} \\ \text{and}}} (9 * 2) + (3 * 6) = 36$

1 6 2

Retain 6 in the answer and carry forward 3 to next step

Therefore, $493 * 162 = $ _____ 66

Step 3.   Perform the next cross multiplication and addition referring to the sequence 12321. The number 3 implies that three digits each from multiplicand and multiplier have to be

multiplied.   4 9 3

$\xrightarrow{\substack{\text{Cross multiplication} \\ \text{and} \\ \text{Addition} \\ \text{and} \\ \text{Add carried forward number}}}$

1 6 2

$(4 * 2) + (9 * 6) + (3 * 1) + 3 = 68$

Retain 8 in the answer and carry forward 6 to next step

Therefore, $493 * 162 = $ _____ 866

Step 4.   Perform the next cross multiplication and addition referring to the sequence 12321.

Cross multiplication
and
Addition
4 9 3   *and*
          Add carried forward number
          $\longrightarrow$

1 6 2

$(4 * 6) + (9 * 1) + 6 = 39$

Retain 9 in the answer and carry forward 3 to next step

Therefore, $493 * 162 = $ ____ 9866

Step 5.   Perform the last cross multiplication referring to the sequence 12321 in the RHS.

Cross multiplication
4 9 3   *and*
          Add carried forward number
          $\longrightarrow (4 * 1) + 3 = 7$

1 6 2

Therefore, $493 * 162 = 79866$

Exercise 6- Solve the any number multiplication problems

1. 264 * 2256	2. 310 * 535	3. 339 * 1239	4. 251 * 1577
5. 333 * 2753	6. 333 * 2753	7. 207 * 40	8. 167 * 46
9. 7694 * 412	10. 9822 * 490	11. 4243 * 622	12. 8749 * 489

Chapter 2.   QUICK AND EASY SUBTRACTION

PERFORMING SUBTRACTION

1. Subtraction is the operation of arriving at the difference $d = x - y$ of two numbers x and y. Here, x is called the minuend, y is called the subtrahend.

2. Two conditions can arise during subtraction

   a. The minuend digit is greater than the subtrahend digit, for example $5 - 3$. Perform direct subtraction in this case $5 - 3 = 2$

   b. The minuend digit is less than the subtrahend digit, for example $3 - 8$. To solve this problem add the complement of subtrahend to the minuend

   $3 - 8 = 3 + 2 = -5$ where 2 is the complement of 8

(1) Perform $5862 - 2160$

   - Quick solution:

	5	8	6	2
−	2	1	6	0
	3	7	0	2

   Therefore, $5862 - 2160 = 3702$

- Detailed Steps:

Direct subtraction

	5	8	6	2
−	2	1	6	0
	$(5-2)$	$(8-1)$	$(6-6)$	$(2-0)$

Implies
$\longrightarrow$

	5	8	6	2
−	2	1	6	0
	3	7	0	2

(2) Perform $5862 - 2971$

- Quick solution:

	5	8	6	2
−	2	9	7	1
	2	8	9	1

Therefore, $5862 - 2971 = 2891$

- Detailed Steps:

Direct subtraction and complement addition for others

	5	8	6	2
−	2	9	7	1

		$(6 + compliment\ of\ 7)$	$(2-1)$

Implies
$\xrightarrow{\quad}$

	5	8	6	2
$-$	2	9	7	1
			$(6+3)$	$(2-1)$

Implies
$\xrightarrow{\quad}$
As the complement of minuend (7) was used in the previous step increment the next subtrahend digit (9) by 1

	5	8	6	2
$-$	2	$9 \xrightarrow{transforms\ to} 10$	7	1
		$(8 + complement\ of\ 10)$	$(6$	$(2$

Implies
$\xrightarrow{\quad}$

	5	8	6	2
$-$	2	9	7	1
		$(8+0)$	$(6+3)$	$(2-1)$

Implies
$\xrightarrow{\quad}$
As the complement of minuend (10) was used in the previous step, increment the next subtrahend digit (2) by 1

	5	8	6	2
$-$	$2 \xrightarrow{transforms\ to} 3$	9	7	1
	$(5-3)$	$(8$	$(6$	$(2$

Implies
$\longrightarrow$

	5	8	6	2
−	2	9	7	1
	2	8	9	1

Therefore, $5862 - 2971 = 2891$

Exercise 7- Perform subtraction

1. **9787 −**	2. **9560 −**	3. **6709 −**	4. **7787 −**
158	**046**	**5967**	**4958**
5. **8387 −**	6. 7522 −	7. 25572 −	8. 52015 −
4421	5682	468	8206

Chapter 3. QUICK AND EASY DIVISION

DIVISION BASICS

Terminology

Dividing 8474 by 2 gives 4237 as the quotient and 0 as the remainder

- Dividend: the number which gets divided. In the above example 8474 is the dividend

- Divisor: the number which divides. In the above example 2 is the divisor

- Quotient: the number of times the dividend is divided by the divisor. 4237 is the quotient in the example

- Remainder: the number which cannot be further divided by the divisor

QUICK DIVISION BY 9s

Rules for dividing by 9s

1. Split the dividend into two columns and place the last digit of the dividend under the remainder column.

2. The first digit of the dividend will form the first digit in the quotient row

3. Add the digit in the quotient row to the next dividend digit to get the next digit in the quotient row

4. Divide the digit in the remainder column by 9 and retain the remainder in the remainder column

5. Carry over the extra digits to the next quotient digit

(1) Perform $\frac{8474}{9}$

- Quick solution:

$$
\begin{array}{ccc|c}
8 & 4 & 7 & 4 \\
\\
& 8 & 12 & 19 \\
\hline
8 & 12 & 19 & 23 \\
\end{array}
$$

Implies
$\longrightarrow$

$$
\begin{array}{ccc|c}
8 & 4 & 7 & 4 \\
\\
& 8 & 12 & 19 \\
\hline
8+1 & 12+2 & 19+2 & \frac{23}{9} = \\
= 9 & = 14 & = 21 & Q2, R5 \\
\end{array}
$$

Therefore, $\frac{8474}{9} = Q941, R5$

- Detailed Steps:

Step 1.   Place the last digit of the multiplicand (4) in the remainder
column

$$8 \quad 4 \quad 7 \ \Big| \qquad\qquad 4$$

Remainder column

Step 2.   Write the first digit of the multiplicand (8) as is in the
quotient digits row.

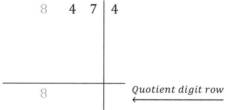

Quotient digit row

Step 3.   Copy the quotient digits row number (8) under the next
dividend digit (4).

8   4   7 | 4

8

8

Step 4.   Add the dividend and the digit under it.

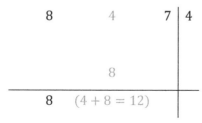

$$8 \quad (4 + 8 = 12)$$

Step 5.   Copy the quotient digits row number under the next

dividend.

```
8    4    7 | 4


     8   12 |
   _____|____
     8   12 |
```

Step 6.   Add the dividend and the digit under it

```
8    4         7    | 4


     8        12
   _____|
     8   12  (7 + 12 = 19)
```

Step 7.   Calculations in the remainder column, copy the quotient

digits row number under the digit in the remainder column

```
8    4    7 | 4


     8   12 | 19
   _____|____
     8   12   19
```

Step 8.   Add the digits under the remainder column

```
8    4    7 |        4


     8   12 |        19
   _____|_____
     8   12   19 | (4 + 19 = 23)
```

Step 9. Divide the digit in the remainder column by 9

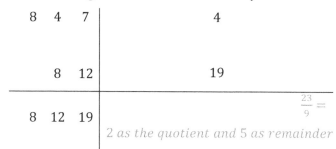

8	4	7		4
	8	12		19

8 12 19 | $\frac{23}{9} =$

2 as the quotient and 5 as remainder

Step 10. Retain the remainder in the quotient row and carry over the quotient to the previous column

8	4	7	4
	8	12	19
8	12	$(19 + 2)$	5

Step 11. Add the digits in the quotient column, retain the unit's digit and carryover the other digits

8	4	7	4
	8	12	19
8	12	$(19 + 2 = 21)$	5

Implies
$\longrightarrow$

8	4	7	4
	8	12	19
8	12 + 2 = 14	1	5

Implies
$\longrightarrow$

8	4	7	4
	8	12	19
8 + 1 = 9	4	1	5

Implies
$\longrightarrow$

8	4	7	4
	8	12	19
9	4	1	5

Therefore,

$$\frac{8474}{9} \xrightarrow{\textit{Results in}} 941 \textit{ as the quotient and 5 as the remainder}$$

Exercise 8 – Quick Division by 9

1. $\dfrac{62184}{9}$ 2. $\dfrac{9852}{9}$ 3. $\dfrac{86121}{9}$ 4. $\dfrac{16392}{9}$

6. $\dfrac{61331}{9}$ 7. $\dfrac{39627}{9}$ 8. $\dfrac{71738}{9}$ 9. $\dfrac{99820}{9}$

11. $\dfrac{86563}{9}$ 12. $\dfrac{74648}{9}$ 13. $\dfrac{37354}{9}$ 14. $\dfrac{75263}{9}$

16. $\dfrac{18261}{9}$ 17. $\dfrac{98280}{9}$ 18. $\dfrac{35857}{9}$ 19. $\dfrac{70168}{9}$

QUICK DIVISION WITH DIVISOR CLOSE TO ITS BASE

Rules for dividing with divisors less than its base

1. Split the dividend into two columns and place the last digits of the dividend under the remainder column. Number of digits in the remainder column should be equal to the number of digits in the divisor

2. If the divisor is less than its base place the complement of the divisor under it. The complement becomes the working divisor

3. If the divisor is more than its base place the difference of the divisor from its base under the divisor. This difference becomes the working divisor. This working divisor will be of negative value.

4. The first digit of the dividend will form the first digit in the quotient row

5. Digits in the quotient row have to be multiplied with the working divisor and added to the next dividend digit to get the next quotient digit

6. If the final number in the remainder column is greater than the actual divisor then divide the number in the remainder column by the divisor and carryover the quotient to the next quotient

(1) Step by step solution: Perform $\frac{36412}{89}$

- Quick solution:

89	3	6	4	1	2
11		3	3		
			9	9	
				17	6

	$3 + 1$	$9 + 1$	$16 + 3$	$\frac{278}{89} =$
	$= 4$	$= 10$	$= 19$	$Q3, R11$

Therefore, $\frac{36412}{89} = Q409, R11$

- Detailed Steps: Note that the divisor 89 is close to base 100 and is less than the base therefore perform the division as follows

Step 1.   Place the last two digits of the multiplicand (12) within the remainder column. Place two digits in the remainder column because the complement of divisor 89 is 11 which is two digits number. Note that 11 will be considered as the working divisor

$$
\begin{array}{c|ccc|cc}
89 & 3 & 6 & 4 & 1 & 2 \\
\end{array}
$$

Workding divisor $\longrightarrow$ 11

↑ *Remainder column*

Step 2.   Write the first digit of the multiplicand (3) as is in the quotient digits row.

$$
\begin{array}{c|ccc|cc}
89 & 3 & 6 & 4 & 1 & 2 \\
11 & & & & & \\
\hline
 & 3 & & & & \\
\end{array}
$$

Step 3.   Multiply the working divisor (11) with the quotient digit (3) and place the product under the next two dividend digits (two because the working divisor is a two digit number)

$$
\begin{array}{c|ccc|cc}
89 & 3 & 6 & 4 & 1 & 2 \\
11 & & 11*3=33 & & & \\
 & & \longrightarrow 3 & 3 & & \\
\hline
 & 3 & & & & \\
\end{array}
$$

Step 4.   Add the next dividend digit and the digit under it

89	3		6		4	1	2
11			3		3		
	3	$(6 + 3 = 9)$					

Step 5.   Multiply the new quotient digit with the working divisor
and place the product under the dividend digits

89	3	6		4		1	2
11		3		3			
			$11*9=99$ $\longrightarrow$ 9		9		
	3	9					

Step 6.   Add the next dividend digit and the digit under it

89	3	6		4		1	2
11		3		3			
				9		9	
	3	9	$(4 + 3 + 9 = 16)$				

In the remainder column, do not perform any addition until the last
digit in the remainder column (2) is reached

Step 7.   Multiply the new quotient digit (16) with the working divisor (11) and place the product under the digits in the remainder column

89	3	6	4		1	2
11		3	3			
			9		9	
					$11*16=176$ $\longrightarrow$ 17	6
	3	9	16			

Note that last digit in the remainder column is reached therefore now add all the digits in the remainder column

Step 8.   Add the digits in the remainder column

89	3	6	4		1	2
11		3	3			
			9		9	
					17	6
	3	9	16	$(12 + 90 + 176 = 278)$		

Step 9.   As the number in the remainder column is 278 which is greater than the divisor 89, divide 278 by 89 to get 3 as the quotient and 11 as the remainder. Retain the remainder (11) in the remainder column and carryover the quotient (3) to the next quotient digit

89	3	6	4		1		2
11		3	3				
			9		9		
					17		6
	3	9	16		$\dfrac{278}{89}$ *Results in* $\longrightarrow$ 3 *as the quotient and*		
					11 *as the remainder*		

Step 10.   Add the quotient digits by performing carryover from one digit to the next to arrive at the final quotient.

89	3	6	4		1	2
11		3	3			
			9		9	
					17	6
	3	9	$(16 + 3 = 19)$		11	

Implies
⟶

89	3	6	4	1	2
11		3	3		
			9	9	
				17	6
	3	$(9 + 1 = 10)$	9	11	

Implies
⟶

89	3	6	4	1	2
11		3	3		
			9	9	
				17	6
	$(3 + 1 = 4)$	0	9	11	

Implies
⟶

89	3	6	4	1	2
11		3	3		
			9	9	
				17	6
	4	0	9	11	

Therefore, $\frac{36412}{89} = 409$ *as quotient and* 11 *as remainder*

(2) Perform $\frac{36412}{112}$

- Quick solution:

112	3	6	4	1	2
-12		-3	-6		
			-3	-6	
				6	0
				12	
	3	$3-1=2$	$10-5=5$		

Therefore, $\frac{36412}{112} \xrightarrow{results\ in} Q325, R12$

- Detailed Steps: Note that the divisor 112 is close to base 100 and is 12 more than the base therefore perform the division as follows

Step 1.   Place the last two digits of the multiplicand (12) within the remainder column. Place two digits in the remainder column because the base here is 100 with two 0s. Note that $100 - 112 = -12$ will be considered as the working divisor

112	3 6 4	1 2
Working divisor $\longrightarrow$		↑ *Remainder column*

Step 2.   Write the first digit of the multiplicand (3) as is in the quotient digits row.

$$
\begin{array}{c|ccc|cc}
112 & 3 & 6 & 4 & 1 & 2 \\
\end{array}
$$

-12

3

Step 3.   Multiply the working divisor (-12) with the quotient digit (3) and place the product under the next two dividend digits (two because the working divisor is a two digit number)

$$
\begin{array}{c|c c c c|c c}
112 & 3 & & 6 & 4 & 1 & 2 \\
\end{array}
$$

-12 $\xrightarrow{-12*3=-36}$ -3 -6

3

Step 4.   Add the next dividend digit and the digit under it

$$
\begin{array}{c|c c c|c c}
112 & 3 & 6 & 4 & 1 & 2 \\
\end{array}
$$

-12 -3 -6

3 $(6 - 3 = 3)$

Step 5.   Multiply the new quotient digit with the working divisor
and place the product under the dividend digits

112	3	6		4	1	2
-12		-3		-6		
			$\xrightarrow{-12*3=-36} -3$	-6		
	3	3				

Step 6.   Add the next dividend digit and the digit under it

112	3	6	4		1	2
-12		-3	-6			
			-3		-6	
	3	3	$(4-6-3=-5)$			

In the remainder column, do not perform any addition until the last
digit in the remainder column (2) is reached

Step 7.   Multiply the new quotient digit (-5) with the working
divisor (-12) and place the product under the digits in the
remainder column

112	3	6	4		1	2
-12		-3	-6			
			-3		-6	
				$\xrightarrow{-12*-5=60} 6$	0	
	3	3	-5			

Note that the operation has reached the last digit in the remainder column. Therefore, now add all the digits in the remainder column

Step 8. Add the digits in the remainder column

112	3	6	4	1	2
−12		−3	−6		
			−3	−6	
				6	0
	3	3	−5	$(12 - 60 + 60 = 12)$	

Step 9. As the number in the remainder column is 12 which is less than 112, retain 12 in the remainder column as remainder and remove the negative sign from the quotient

112	3	6	4	1	2
−12		−3	−6		
			−3	−6	
				6	0
	3	3	−5	12	

Step 10.   Carry forward 1 from the previous quotient digit to remove the negative sign from the quotient digit (-5).

112	3	6	4	1	2
−12		−3	−6		
			−3	−6	
				6	0
					12
	3	$(3-1$ $=2)\xrightarrow{carry\ forward\ 1}$	$(10-5$ $=5)$		

Implies $\longrightarrow$

112	3	6	4	1	2
−12		−3	−6		
			−3	−6	
				6	0
					12
	3	2	5	12	

Therefore, $\dfrac{36412}{112} \xrightarrow{results\ in} 325\ as\ quotient\ and\ 12\ as\ remainder$

Exercise 9 – Quick Division by Divisor close to its Base

1. $\dfrac{55368}{89}$ 2. $\dfrac{95896}{89}$ 3. $\dfrac{61886}{104}$ 4. $\dfrac{62998}{115}$

6. $\dfrac{76690}{89}$ 7. $\dfrac{50747}{112}$ 8. $\dfrac{33645}{93}$ 9. $\dfrac{36863}{104}$

ANY NUMBER DIVISION USING FLAGGED DIVISORS

Rules for dividing with any divisors

1. Split the divisor into the working divisor and the flag. The working divisor will always be 1 digit and all the other digits will be the flag. Consider the example

$$\frac{36412}{132}; \; Divisor \; 132 \xrightarrow[working \; divisor]{Splits \; into} 1^{32} \xleftarrow{flag}$$

2. Split the dividend into two columns and the number of digits in the last remainder column should be equal to the number of digits in the flag

$$
\begin{array}{ccc|cc}
3 & 6 & 4 & 1 & 2
\end{array}
$$

3. Divide the first digit of the dividend by the working divisor and write the quotient in the quotient row and move the remainder before the next dividend digit. This new dividend digit becomes the gross dividend from which the working dividend is deduced.

4. Multiply the quotient digit with the flag and subtract the same from the gross dividend to get the working dividend.

5. Divide the working dividend by the divisor and write the quotient in the quotient column and the remainder will form the first digit of the gross dividend.

6. Continue the steps till the last digit is completed.

(1) Perform $\frac{54225}{46}$ with required correction

- Quick solution:

4^6	5	$_1 4$	$_0$ $_4 2$	$_0$ $_4$ $_8 2$	$_0$ $_4$ $_8 5$	$_1$ $_5 0$	$_2 0$
				$-54-48$	-60	-54	0
			-4	-42	-54	-48	
		-6	-6		-48		
	8	36	40	37	2	20	
	1	$2\,1$	$9\,8\,7$	$10\,9\,8$	$9\,8$	0	5

- Detailed Steps: Note that the divisor 46 is a two digit number therefore the division will be performed with one flag; 4 will be the working divisor and 6 will be the flag

Step 1.   Split the dividend into the quotient column and the remainder column. Number of digits in the remainder column should be equal to the number of digits in the flag (1)

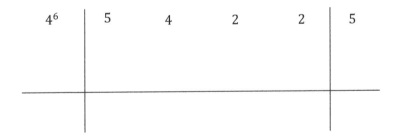

4^6	5	4	2	2	5

Step 2.   Following the previous example we now arrive at the negative working dividend (-10)

4^6	5	$_14$	$_02$	2	5
		-6	-12		
		8	-10		
	1	2			

Step 3. To avoid the negative working dividend go back one step and reduce the quotient by 1. Therefore instead of 2 the new quotient will be 1. $\xrightarrow{Implies}$

4^6	5	$_14$		2	2	5
		-6				
		8				
	1	2 $\xrightarrow{Quotient\ reduced\ by\ 1}$ 1				

Step 4. Perform the subsequent steps as in the previous example

4^6	5	$_14$	$_42$	$_82$	$_85$	$_50$	$_20$
		-6	-6	-42	-48	-48	0
		8	36	40	37	2	20
	1	1	7	8	8	0	5

Therefore, $\dfrac{54225}{46} = 1178.805$

(2) Step by step solution: Perform $\dfrac{88770}{542}$

- Quick solution:

5^{42}	8	$_3 8$	$_4 7$	$_{\mathbf{1}}{}_6 7$	$_3{}_8 0$
	4	26	~~28~~ 24	~~38~~ 34
	34	21	43	46
			~~8~~ 7	8
0	1	6	4 3	

Therefore, $\dfrac{88770}{542} = 163.78$

- Detailed steps:

Note that the divisor 542 is a three digit number therefore the division will be performed with two flags, 5 will be the divisor and 42 will be the flag

Step 1.   Split the divisor into the working divisor (WD 5) and flag
(f 42)

5^{42}	8	8	7	7	0

Step 2.   Calculate the first quotient digit (Q) digit under the gross dividend by dividing the gross dividend (GD) by the working divisor (WD). Move the remainder (R) as prefix to the next GD digit (8).

$WD\ 5^{f\ 42}$	$GD\ 8$		8	7	7	0
	$\dfrac{GD\ 8}{WD\ 5} = Q\ 1, R3$					

Implies $\longrightarrow$

$WD\ 5^{f\ 42}$	$GD\ 8$	$_{R\ 3}8$	7	7	0
	$Q\ 1$				

Step 3.   Find the next working dividend (d)

3.1. Find the digit under the next GD (38). Perform cross multiplication and addition between the flag and the quotient digits.

5^{f42}	8	$GD\ {}_{3}8$		7	7	0
		Cross multiplication and addition $\longrightarrow$				
		$f4\quad f2$				
		$Q0\quad Q1$				
		$(f4 * Q1) + (f2 * Q0) = 4$				
$Q0$	$Q1$					

3.2. Perform subtraction between the GD and the arrived number to arrive at the next working dividend (d)

5^{f42}	8	$GD\ _38$	7	7	0
		4			
		$38 - 4 = d\ 34$			
$Q0$	$Q1$				

Step 4.   Calculate the next quotient digit (Q) by dividing the dividend (d) by the working divisor 5

5^{42}	8	$_38$	7	7	0
		4			
		34			
0	$Q1$	$\dfrac{34}{5} \xrightarrow{Results\ in} Q6, R4$			

Implies
$\longrightarrow$

5^{42}	8	$_38$	$_{R4}7$	7	0
		4			
		34			
0	1	$Q6$			

Step 5.   Perform in similar steps to arrive at the quotient and the remainder

5^{42}	8	$_38$	$_{R4}7$	7	0
			Cross multiplication		
			and		
	4	$f4$ $f2$ $\xrightarrow{\;addition\;}$			
		$q1$ $q6$			
		$(f4 * q6) + (f2 * q1) = 26$			
	34				
0	$Q1$ $Q6$				

Implies $\longrightarrow$

5^{42}	8	$_38$	$_47$	7	0
	4		26		
	34		$47 - 26 = 21$		
0	$Q1$	$Q6$			

Implies $\longrightarrow$

5^{42}	8	$_38$	$_47$	7	0
	4		26		
	34		21		
0	$Q1$	$Q6$	$\frac{21}{5} \xrightarrow{\;Results\;in\;} Q4, R1$		

61

Implies
$\longrightarrow$

5^{42}	8	$_38$		$_47$		7	0
		4		26			
		34		21			

0	Q1	Q6				

Q4 used instead of Q3 to avoid negative quotient

$Q3 \xrightarrow{\hspace{3cm}} Q4$

Implies
$\longrightarrow$

5^{42}	8	$_38$		$_47$		7	0
		4		26			
		34		21			

0	Q1	Q6

$Q3 \xrightarrow{\text{Implies}} 5 * 3 = 15$

$Remainder(r) = 21 - 15$

$= 6$

Implies
$\longrightarrow$

5^{42}	8	$_38$	$_47$	$_67$	0
		4	26		
		34	21		

0	Q1	Q6	Q3

Implies
$\longrightarrow$

$_5{}^{42}$	8	$_3 8$	$_4 7$		$_6 7$		0
		4	26	$f4$ $f2$			
				$q6$ $q3$			
		34	21				
0	Q1	Q6	Q3				

*Cross multiplication
and
addition*
$\longrightarrow$

$(f4 * q3) + (f2 * q6) = 24$

Implies
$\longrightarrow$

$_5{}^{42}$	8	$_3 8$	$_4 7$	$_6 7$	0
		4	26	24	
		34	21	33	
0	Q1	Q6	Q3		

Implies
$\longrightarrow$

$_5{}^{42}$	8	$_3 8$	$_4 7$	$_6 7$	$_8 0$
		4	26	24	
		34	21	43	
0	Q1	Q6	Q3		R7

Implies
$\longrightarrow$

5^{42}	8	$_3 8$	$_4 7$	$_6 7$	$_8 0$
				24	*Cross multiplication*
					and
		4	26		$f4 \quad f2 \quad \xrightarrow{addition}$
					$q3 \quad q7$
					$(f4 * q7) + (f2 * q3) = 34$
		34	21	43	
0	Q1	Q6	Q3	R7	

Implies
$\longrightarrow$

5^{42}	8	$_3 8$	$_4 7$	$_6 7$	$_8 0$
		4	26	24	34
		34	21	43	46
0	Q1	Q6	Q3	R7	R8

Therefore, $\dfrac{88770}{542} = 163.78$

Exercise 10 – Any Number division using flagged divisor

1. $\dfrac{163258}{4241}$	2. $\dfrac{326978}{9726}$	3. $\dfrac{976683}{7474}$	4. $\dfrac{583782}{1578}$
6. $\dfrac{473674}{5772}$	7. $\dfrac{322878}{1029}$	8. $\dfrac{60301}{6689}$	9. $\dfrac{376280}{1322}$
11. $\dfrac{536706}{4836}$	12. $\dfrac{841196}{5834}$	13. $\dfrac{504876}{2359}$	14. $\dfrac{19711}{2199}$

Chapter 4.   CHECK FOR ERRORS IN

CALCULATIONS

INTRODUCTION TO DIGITAL ROOTS

What are digital roots?

1. Digital root for any number is the sum of its digits

2. Digital root of any number is always between 1 and 9

(1) Find the digital roots of 37601

$Digital\ root\ of\ 37601 = DR(37601) = 3 + 7 + 6 + 0 + 1 = 17$

$\xrightarrow{Solving\ further} DR(17) = 1 + 7 = 8$

Therefore, $DR(37601) = 8$

(2) Check if the equation $34534 + 45659 = 80193$ is correct

- Quick solution: $DR(34534) + DR(45659) = DR(80193)$

  $DR(19) + DR(29) = DR(21) \xrightarrow{Solving\ further} 1 + 2 = 3$

  Therefore, the equation $34534 + 45659 = 80193$ is correct

- Detailed steps:

Step 1.   Find the DR of each number in the LHS and the RHS

1.1. $DR(34534) = 3 + 4 + 5 + 3 + 4 = 19$

$\xrightarrow{Solving\ further} DR(19) = 1 + 9 = 10$

$\xrightarrow{Solving\ further} DR(10) = 1 + 0 = 1$

Therefore, $DR(34534) = 1$

1.2. $DR(45659) = 4 + 5 + 6 + 5 + 9 = 29$

$\xrightarrow{Solving\ further} DR(29) = 2 + 9 = 11$

$\xrightarrow{Solving\ further} DR(11) = 1 + 1 = 2$

Therefore, $DR(45659) = 2$

1.3. $DR(80193) = 8 + 0 + 1 + 9 + 3 = 21$

$\xrightarrow{Solving\ further} DR(21) = 2 + 1 = 3$

Therefore, $DR(80193) = 3$

Step 2.   Check if $DR(34534) + DR(45659) = DR(80193)$

$LHS = DR(34534) + DR(45659) = 1 + 2 = 3$

$RHS = DR(80193) = 3$

As the LHS is equal to the RHS, therefore the equation

$34534 + 45659 = 80193$ is correct

(3) Check if the equation $42 * 77 = 3134$ is correct

- Quick solution: $DR(42) * DR(77) = DR(3134)$

$DR(6 * 5) = DR(2) \xrightarrow{Solving\ further} 3 \neq 2$

Therefore, the equation $42 * 77 = 3134$ is not correct

- Detailed steps:

Step 1.   Check if $DR(42) * DR(77) = DR(3134)$

1.1. $LHS = DR(42) * DR(77) \xrightarrow{Solving\ further}$

$DR(6) * DR(14)$

$\xrightarrow{Solving\ further}$

$DR(6) * DR(5) \xrightarrow{Solving\ further} DR(6 * 5) = 3$

1.2. $RHS = DR(3134) = DR(11) = DR(2) = 2$

Step 2.   Check if the LHS value equals the RHS value

$LHS = 3$

$RHS = 2$

As LHS $\neq$ RHS, the equation $42 * 77 = 3134$ is not correct

Exercise 11 – Checking for Errors

1. $\dfrac{868168}{2933} = 296$	2. $\dfrac{148070}{8710} =$ **16**	3. $\dfrac{483828}{1753} =$ **270**
5. $326 + 61754 =$ **62080**	6. $51970 +$ $31097 =$ 84067	7. $93233 -$ $84134 =$ 9099
9. $1848 * 2869 =$ **5311912**	10. $7766 *$ $79 =$ 613514	

Chapter 5.   WORKING WITH FRACTIONS

DIVISION OF FRACTION BASICS

Conditions for quick division of fractions

- Dividend or numerator should be less than the divisor or the denominator

- Divisor is a small 2 or 3 digit number

- Divisor ends with 1, 6, 7, 8, and 9

DIVISORS ENDING WITH 1, 6, 7, 8, and 9

Rules for dividing with 1, 6, 7, 8, and 9

1. Convert the fraction to its auxiliary function

2. Perform the division of the auxiliary function

(1) Convert $\frac{1}{19}$ to its decimal form

- Quick solution:

$$AF\left(\frac{1}{19+1}\right) \xrightarrow{Implies} \frac{0.1}{2} \xrightarrow{results\ in} 0._10_05_12_06_03_11_15_17_18$$

Therefore, $\frac{1}{19} = 0.052631578$

- Detailed steps: Note that the divisor (19) is ending in 9 and the dividend (1) is less than the divisor (19). Convert the problem to its auxiliary function and solve it.

Step 1. Convert $\frac{1}{19}$ to its auxiliary function (AF)

$$AF\left(\frac{1}{19}\right) \xrightarrow{Implies} \frac{1}{19+1} = \frac{1}{20} = \frac{0.1}{2}$$

Add 1 to the denominator 19 and remove 0 from the denominator 20

Step 2. Perform the division of the auxiliary function $\frac{0.1}{2}$

Introduce decimal in the solution, $\frac{0.1}{2} \xrightarrow{results\ in} 0.\,;$

$0.\,_10 \xleftarrow{Result\ of\ division} \frac{1}{2} = Q0, R1;$

$0.\,_10\,_05 \xleftarrow{Result\ of\ division} \frac{10}{2} = Q5, R0;$

$0.\,_10\,_05\,_12 \xleftarrow{Result\ of\ division} \frac{05}{2} = Q2, R1;$

$\xrightarrow{Performing\ similarly} 0.\,_10\,_05\,_12\,_06\,_03\,_11\,_15\,_17\,_18$

$Therefore, \frac{1}{19} = 0.052631578$

(2) Convert $\frac{6}{39}$ to its decimal form

- Quick solution: $AF\left(\frac{6}{39+1}\right) \xrightarrow{Implies} \frac{0.6}{4} \xrightarrow{results\ in} 0.\,_21\,_15\,_33\,_18\,_24\,_06\,_21$

  Therefore, $\frac{6}{39} = 0.1538461$

- Detailed steps: Note that the divisor (39) is ending in 9 and the dividend (6) is less than the divisor. Convert the problem to its auxiliary function and solve it.

Step 1. Convert $\frac{6}{39}$ to its auxiliary function (AF)

$$AF\left(\frac{6}{39}\right) \xrightarrow{Implies} \frac{6}{39+1} = \frac{6}{40} = \frac{0.6}{4}$$

Add 1 to the denominator 39 and remove 0 from the denominator 40

Step 2. Perform the division of the auxiliary function $\frac{0.6}{4}$

Introduce decimal in the solution, $\frac{0.6}{4} \xrightarrow{results\ in} 0.\ ;$

$$0._21 \xleftarrow{Result\ of\ division} \frac{6}{4} = Q1, R2;$$

$$0._21_15 \xleftarrow{Result\ of\ division} \frac{21}{4} = Q5, R1;$$

$$0._21_15_33 \xleftarrow{Result\ of\ division} \frac{15}{4} = Q3, R3;$$

$$0._21_15_33_18 \xleftarrow{Result\ of\ division} \frac{33}{4} = Q8, R1;$$

$$0._21_15_33_18_24 \xleftarrow{Result\ of\ division} \frac{18}{4} = Q4, R2;$$

Therefore, performing similarly $\frac{6}{39} = 0.1538461$

(3) Convert $\frac{27}{58}$ to its decimal form

- Quick solution: $AF\left(\frac{27}{58+2}\right) \xrightarrow{Implies} \frac{2.7}{6} \xrightarrow{results\ in} 0._34_26_25_05_41_07_22$

  Therefore, $\frac{27}{58} = 0.4655172$

- Detailed steps: Note that the divisor (58) is ending in 8 and the dividend (27) is less than the divisor. Convert the problem to its auxiliary function and solve it. Unlike in the previous example when the divisor ends with 8 as in this example, the working dividend will be the dividend arrived (from the previous step) + the last digit of the dividend. If the arrived dividend is 34 then the working dividend will be $34 + 4 = 38$, if the arrived dividend is 48 then the working dividend will be $48 + 8 = 56$

Step 1.   Convert $\frac{27}{58}$ to its auxiliary function (AF)

$$AF\left(\frac{27}{58}\right) \xrightarrow{Implies} \frac{27}{58+2} = \frac{27}{60} = \frac{2.7}{6}$$

Add 2 to the denominator 58 and remove 0 from the denominator 60

Step 2.   Perform the division of the auxiliary function $\frac{0.6}{4}$

Introduce decimal in the answer $\xrightarrow{yields} \frac{2.7}{6} = 0.$

Perform $\frac{27}{6}$ and write the quotient (4) and the remainder (3) as the next working dividend (34)

$$\xrightarrow{Implies} \frac{2.7}{6} = 0._34$$

As the initial divisor 58 ends in 8 evaluate the new working dividend by adding the arrived working dividend (34) to the last digit of the arrived working dividend (4). Therefore, $34 + 1 =$ 38   becomes the new working dividend, therefore perform $\frac{38}{6}$ and write the quotient (6) and the remainder (2)

$$\xrightarrow{Implies} \frac{2.7}{6} = 0._34_26$$

Now instead of 26, $26 + 6 = 32$ becomes the new working dividend, therefore perform $\frac{32}{6}$ and write the quotient (5) and the remainder (2)

$$\xrightarrow{Implies} \frac{2.7}{6} = 0._34_26_25$$

Similarly arrive at the quotient for any number of decimals

$\xrightarrow{Implies} \dfrac{2.7}{6} = 0._34_26_25_05_41_07_22$

Therefore, $\dfrac{27}{58} = 0.4655172$

(4) Convert $\dfrac{14}{87}$ to its decimal form

- Quick solution: $AF\left(\dfrac{14}{87+3}\right) \xrightarrow{Implies} \dfrac{1.4}{9} \xrightarrow{results\ in} 0._51_85_510_88_811$

  Therefore, $\dfrac{14}{87} = 0.16091$

- Detailed steps: Note that the divisor (87) is ending in 7 and the dividend (14) is less than the divisor. Convert the problem to its auxiliary function and solve it. In cases where the divisor ends in 7, the working dividend will be the dividend arrived (from the previous step) + twice the last digit of the dividend arrived. If the arrived dividend is 34 then the working dividend will be $34 + (2 * 4) = 42$

Step 1.   Convert $\dfrac{14}{87}$ to its auxiliary function (AF)

$AF\left(\dfrac{14}{87}\right) \xrightarrow{Implies} \dfrac{14}{87+3} = \dfrac{14}{90} = \dfrac{1.4}{9}$

Add 3 to the denominator 87 and remove 0 from the denominator 90

Step 2.   Perform the division of the auxiliary function $\dfrac{1.4}{9}$

$Introduce\ decimal \xrightarrow{yields} \dfrac{1.4}{9} = 0.$

Perform $\dfrac{1.4}{9}$ and write the quotient (1) and the remainder (5)

$\xrightarrow{Implies} \dfrac{1.4}{9} = 0._51$

Now instead of 51 as the working dividend, $51 + (2 *$

$last\ digit\ in51) \xrightarrow{Implies} 51 + (2 * 1) = 53$

becomes the working dividend, therefore perform $\frac{53}{9}$ and write the quotient (5) and the remainder (8)

$\xrightarrow{Implies} \frac{1.4}{9} = 0._{5}1_{8}5$

Similarly instead of 85 as the working dividend,

$85 + (2 * last\ digit\ in\ 85) \xrightarrow{Implies} 85 + (2 * 5) = 95$

becomes the working dividend, therefore perform $\frac{95}{9}$ and write the quotient (10) and the remainder (5)

$\xrightarrow{Implies} \frac{1.4}{9} = 0._{5}1_{8}5_{5}10$

In this case the dividend arrived 5 10 is written as $50 + 10 = 60$

Now instead of $(50 + 10)$ 60 as the working dividend

$60 + (2 * 10) = 80$ becomes the working dividend, therefore perform $\frac{80}{9}$ and write the quotient (8) and the remainder (8)

$\xrightarrow{Implies} \frac{1.4}{9} = 0._{5}1_{8}5_{5}10_{8}8$

The working dividend now is $88 + (2 * 8) = 104$. Performing $\frac{104}{9}$ arrive at 11 as the quotient and 8 as the remainder.

$\xrightarrow{Implies} \frac{1.4}{9} = 0._{5}1_{8}5_{5}10_{8}8_{8}11$

Remove all the remainder digits and retain only the quotient digits

$\xrightarrow{Implies} \frac{1.4}{9} = 0.\ 1\ 5\ 10\ 8\ 11$

Retaining only the unit digits at each position and carrying over the rest to the previous digits for the final solution

Therefore, $\frac{14}{87} = 0.16091$

(5) Convert $\frac{45}{46}$ to its decimal form

- Quick solution: $AF\left(\frac{45}{46+4}\right) \xrightarrow{Implies} \frac{4.5}{5} \xrightarrow{results\ in} 0._09_17_37_311$

  Therefore, $\frac{45}{46} = 0.9781$

- Detailed steps: Note that the divisor (46) is ending in 6 and the dividend (45) is less than the divisor. Convert the problem to its auxiliary function and solve it. In cases where the divisor ends in 6, the working dividend is calculated as

$$WD =$$
$$divident\ from\ previous\ step$$
$$+(3 * last\ digit\ of\ dividend)$$

Step 1.   Convert $\frac{45}{46}$ to its auxiliary function (AF)

$$AF\left(\frac{45}{46}\right) \xrightarrow{Implies} \frac{45}{46+4} = \frac{45}{50} = \frac{4.5}{5}$$

Add 4 to the denominator 46 and remove 0 from the denominator 50

Step 2.   Perform the division of the auxiliary function $\frac{4.5}{5}$

Introduce the decimal

$$\xrightarrow{Implies} \frac{4.5}{5} = 0.$$

Perform $\frac{45}{5}$ to get 9 as the quotient and 0 as the remainder

$$\xrightarrow{Implies} \frac{4.5}{5} = 0._09$$

Instead of 09 as the working dividend,

$$09 + (3 * last\ digit\ in\ 09) = 09 + (3 * 9) = 36$$

becomes the working dividend, therefore perform $\frac{36}{5}$ to get 7 as the quotient and 1 as the remainder

$\xrightarrow{Implies} \frac{4.5}{5} = 0._09_17$

Again instead of 17 as the working dividend,

$17 + (3 * last\ digit\ in\ 17) = 17 + (3 * 7) = 38$

becomes the working dividend, therefore perform $\frac{38}{5}$ to get 7 as

the quotient and 3 as the remainder

$\xrightarrow{Implies} \frac{4.5}{5} = 0._09_17_37$

Instead of 37 as the working dividend,

$37 + (3 * last\ digit\ in\ 37) = 37 + (3 * 7) = 58$

becomes the working dividend, therefore perform $\frac{58}{5}$ to get 11 as

the quotient and 3 as the remainder

$\xrightarrow{Implies} \frac{4.5}{5} = 0._09_17_37_311$

By removing all the remainder digits and retaining only the

quotient digits arrive at $\xrightarrow{Implies} \frac{4.5}{5} = 0.9\ 7\ 7\ 11$

Retaining only the unit digits and carrying over the rest to the

previous digits to arrive at the final answer.

Therefore, $\frac{45}{46} = 0.9781$

(6) Convert $\frac{5}{31}$ to its decimal form

- Quick solution: $AF\left(\frac{5-1}{31-1}\right) \xrightarrow{Implies} \frac{0.4}{3} \xrightarrow{results\ in} 0._11\,^8_06\,^3_01\,^8$

  Therefore, $\frac{5}{31} = 0.161$

- Detailed steps: Note that the divisor (31) is ending in 1 and the dividend (5) is less than the divisor. Convert the problem to its auxiliary function and solve it. In cases where the divisor ends in

1, the working dividend will be arrived at by subtracting the last digit of the arrived dividend by 9. If the arrived dividend is 34 then the working dividend will be $30 + (9 - 4) = 35$

Step 1.   Convert $\dfrac{5}{31}$ to its auxiliary function (AF)

$$AF\left(\dfrac{5}{31}\right) \xrightarrow{Implies} \dfrac{4}{31-1} = \dfrac{4}{30} = \dfrac{0.4}{3}$$

Subtract 1 from the numerator and the denominator and remove 0 from the divisor

Step 2.   Ignore the decimal in the numerator 0.4 and introduce decimal in the solution

$$\dfrac{4}{3} \xrightarrow[\text{in the solution}]{Introduce\ decimal} 0.$$

Step 3.   Perform the division of the auxiliary function $\dfrac{4}{3}$

Perform $\dfrac{4}{3}$ to get 1 as the quotient and 1 as the remainder

$$\dfrac{4}{3} \xrightarrow[\text{Remainder of}]{\substack{Quotient \\ and}} 0._1 1$$

Find the unit's digit of the working dividend. Perform

$$(9 - quotient\ digit) \xrightarrow{Implies} 9 - 1 = 8$$

Append 8 to the working solution

$$\dfrac{4}{3} \xrightarrow{Working\ dividend} 0._1 1\ ^8 \text{, therefore 18 becomes the next WD}$$

Perform $\dfrac{18}{3}$ to arrive at 6 as the quotient and 0 as the remainder

$$\dfrac{4}{3} \xrightarrow[\text{Remainder of}]{\substack{Quotient \\ and}} 0._1 1\ ^8{}_0 6$$

Find the unit's digit of the working dividend. Perform

$$(9 - quotient\ digit) \xrightarrow{Implies} 9 - 6 = 3$$

Append 3 to the working solution

$$\frac{4}{3} \xrightarrow{Working\ dividend} 0._11^8{}_06^{\ 3}\text{ , therefore 03 becomes the next}$$

WD

Perform $\frac{03}{3}$ to arrive at 1 as the quotient and 0 as the remainder

$$\frac{4}{3} \xrightarrow[\text{and}]{\substack{Quotient\ and\ Remainder\ of}} 0._11^8{}_06^{\ 3}{}_01$$

Find the unit's digit of the working dividend. Perform

$$(9 - quotient\ digit) \xrightarrow{Implies} 9 - 1 = 8$$

Append 8 to the working solution

$$\frac{4}{3} \xrightarrow{Working\ dividend} 0._11^8{}_06^{\ 3}{}_01^{\ 8}$$

Removing all the remainder digits and retaining only the quotient digits we arrive at 0. 1612 as the answer.

Therefore, $\frac{5}{31} = 0.161$

Exercise 12 – Working with Fractions

1. $\frac{5}{41}$	2. $\frac{12}{57}$	3. $\frac{3}{9}$	4. $\frac{14}{17}$
5. $\frac{8}{18}$	6. $\frac{27}{28}$	7. $\frac{10}{19}$	8. $\frac{1}{18}$
9. $\frac{2}{19}$	10. $\frac{7}{11}$	11. $\frac{14}{19}$	12. $\frac{7}{78}$

DIVISORS ENDING WITH 2, 3, 4, and 5

Convert fractions with denominators ending in 2, 3, 4, and 5 to its decimal form

To convert such fractions in decimals, first multiply the numerator and the denominator with a suitable number to make the denominator end with 1, 6, 7, 8, or 9 and perform the conversion to decimals as done in the previous examples.

Use the following table to convert the denominator to 1, 6, 7, 8, or 9

Denominators	Fraction example	Suitable number to multiply	Final fraction
2	$\frac{5}{22}$	3	$\frac{5}{22} * \frac{3}{3} = \frac{15}{66}$
3	$\frac{8}{13}$	2	$\frac{8}{13} * \frac{2}{2} = \frac{16}{26}$
4	$\frac{3}{24}$	2	$\frac{3}{24} * \frac{2}{2} = \frac{6}{48}$
5	$\frac{4}{35}$	2	$\frac{4}{35} * \frac{2}{2} = \frac{8}{70}$

Chapter 6.   SQUARES AND SQUARE ROOTS

SQUARES OF NUMBERS ENDING IN 5

To find the square of any number ending in 5 split the number into 1st part and the 2nd part. The second part consists only of 5 and the 1st part consists of the rest of the numbers. For the solution multiply the first part of the number with its successor and then append 25 at the end to the product.

(1) Find the square of 15

- Quick solution: $1 * 2 \ 25 = 2 \ 25$

    Therefore, $15^2 = 225$

- Detailed steps:

Step 1.   Split the number 15

$$15 \xrightarrow{Split\ into} 1\ and\ 5$$

Step 2.   Multiply the first digit (1) with its successor (2) and write the product

$$1 * 2 = 2$$

The number 2 becomes the LHS part of the answer

Step 3.   Write 25 as the RHS part of the answer

Step 4.   Combine the LHS part (2) and RHS part (25) for the answer

$$\therefore 15^2 = 225$$

(2) Find the square of 135

- Quick solution: $13 * 14 \ \ 25 = 182 \ \ 25$

    Therefore, $135^2 = 18225$

- Detailed steps:

Step 1.   Split the number 135 into 13 and 5

$$135 \xrightarrow{Split\ into} 13\ and\ 5$$

Step 2.   Multiply the first set of digits (13) with its successor (14) and write the product

$$13 * 14 = 182$$

The number 182 becomes the LHS part of the answer

Step 3.   Write 25 as the RHS part of the answer

Step 4.   Combine the LHS part (2) and the RHS part (25) for the answer

$$\therefore 135^2 = 18225$$

SQUARES OFANY NUMBERS

Understand the concept of duplex of any number

Numbε	Denotion	Duplex of Number	Example
a	$D(a)$	a^2	$D(3) \xrightarrow{Implies} 3^2 = 9$
ab	$D(ab)$	$2*a*b$	$D(64) \xrightarrow{Implies} 2*6*4 = 48$
abc	$D(abc)$	$(2*a*c) + b^2$	$D(531) \xrightarrow{Implies} (2*5*1) + 3^2 = 19$
$abcd$	$D(abcd)$	$(2*a*d) +(2*b*c)$	$D(7014) \xrightarrow{Implies} (2*7*4) + (2*0*1) = 56$

Square of any number

Numbε	Denotion
a^2	$D(a)$
ab^2	$D(a)D(ab)D(b)$
abc^2	$D(a)D(ab)D(abc)D(bc)D(c)$

$abcd^2$	$D(a)D(ab)D(abc)D(abcd)D(bcd)D(cd)D(d)$

(1) Find the square of 13

- Quick solution: $D(1)$ $D(13)$ $D(3) = 1$ 6   9

  Therefore, $13^2 = 169$

- Detailed steps:

Step 1.   Write the duplex of the number

$$D(13) \xrightarrow{Implies} D(1)\ D(13)\ D(3)$$

where each duplex forms the digit in the answer

Step 2.   Resolve the first duplex to get the first digit in the answer

$$D(1) \xrightarrow{Implies} 1^2 = 1$$

Step 3.   Resolve the next duplex to get the next digit in the answer

$$D(13) \xrightarrow{Implies} 2*1*3 = 6$$

Step 4.   Resolve the last duplex to get the last digit in the answer

$$D(3) \xrightarrow{Implies} 3^2 = 9$$

Step 5.   Combine all the digits in the answer for the final solution.

  Therefore, $13^2 = 169$

(2) Find the square of 4709

- Quick solution:

  $D(4)$ $D(47)$ $D(470)$ $D(4709)$ $D(709)$ $D(09)$ $D(9)$

  $= 16$ 56   49   72   126   0   81 $\xrightarrow{Results\ in} 22174681$

  Therefore, $4709^2 = 22174681$

- Detailed steps:

Step 1.   Write the duplex of the number

$D(4709)$

$\xrightarrow{Implies} D(4)\ D(47)\ D(470)\ D(4709)\ D(709)\ D(09)\ D(9)$

where each duplex forms the digit in the answer

Step 2.   Resolve the first duplex to get the first digit in the answer

$D(4) \xrightarrow{Implies} 4^2 = 16$

Step 3.   Resolve the subsequent duplexes to get the digits in the

answer $D(47) \xrightarrow{Implies} 2*4*7 = 56$

$D(470) \xrightarrow{Implies} (2*4*0) + 7^2\ = 49$

$D(4709) \xrightarrow{Implies} (2*4*9) + (2*7*0)\ = 72$

$D(709) \xrightarrow{Implies} (2*7*9) + 0^2\ = 126$

$D(09) \xrightarrow{Implies} (2*0*9)\ = 0$

$D(9) \xrightarrow{Implies} 9^2\ = 81$

Step 4.   Combine all the digits in the answer

$\xrightarrow{Implies}$ 16; 56; 49; 72; 126; 0; 81

Step 5.   Retain one digit at each position from the RHS and carry-

over the extra numbers to arrive at the final solution

$\xrightarrow{Implies}$ 22174681 *in answer*

Therefore, $4709^2 = 22174681$

Exercise 13 – Squares of any Numbers

1. 65^2	2. 235^2	3. 85^2	4. 574^2
6. 9646^2	7. 4224^2	8. 9008^2	9. 7640^2

SQUARE ROOTS OFANY NUMBERS

Steps for finding the Square root of any number

1. Identify if the number of digits in the number is even or odd

2. If the number of digits in the number is odd then consider the first digit as the Working Digit (WD)

3. If the number of digits in the number is even then consider the consider the first two digits as the Working Digits (WD)

4. Find the highest Square Root (SR) below the WD and write that below the WD

5. The SR below the working digit becomes the first digit of the answer (square root)

6. Multiply the SR by 2 and write the result as the Divisor (Di)

7. Find the rest of the digits in the square root by division

8. The Actual Dividend (AD) is obtained by subtracting the duplex from the Gross Dividend (GD)

9. Finally mark the decimal in the square root depending on the number of digits in the initial number

(1) Find the square root of 2209

- Quick solution:

	22	$_{22-16=6}$0	$_4$9
		56	−49
8			0
	4	7	. 0

$Therefore, \sqrt{2209} = 47$

- Detailed steps:

Step 1.   The number 2209 has even number of digits (4).
Therefore, n=4 and the Working Digit (WD) is 22

Step 2.   The highest square below 22 is 16, therefore the highest square root below 22 is 4 ($\sqrt{16} = 4$). Write this 4 (SR) as the first digit of the answer (square root of 2209).

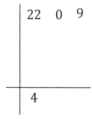

Step 3.   Multiply the SR (4) with 2 and write that as the divisor (8).

85

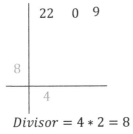

$$Divisor = 4 * 2 = 8$$

Step 4.   For the next Gross Dividend (GD), prefix the difference of WD (22) and the highest square (16) to the next working digit (0) in the problem.

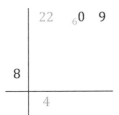

$$first\ digit\ in\ GD = 22 - 4^2 = 6$$

Step 5.   Divide the next gross dividend (60) by the divisor (8) and write the quotient as the next digit in the answer (square root) and transfer the remainder as a prefix to the next working digit in the problem.

$$
\begin{array}{l}
\hspace{1.2cm} 22 \hspace{0.8cm} {}_6 0 \hspace{0.6cm} {}_4 9 \\
\hspace{2.2cm} -56 \\
8 \\
\hline
\hspace{0.8cm} 4 \hspace{0.8cm} 7
\end{array}
$$

$$60/8 = 7\ as\ quotient, 4\ as\ the\ remainder$$

Step 6.   For the next working dividend, subtract the gross dividend from the duplex of the square root. Ignore the first digit in the square root while calculating the gross dividend.

$$
\begin{array}{c|ccc}
 & 22 & {}_6 0 & {}_4 9 \\
 & & -56 & -49 \\
8 & & & \\
\hline
 & 4 & 7 & \\
\end{array}
$$

$$D(7) \xrightarrow{Implies} 7^2 = 49$$

Step 7.   Subtracting the duplex (49) from the gross dividend (49) gives the next working dividend (0). Divide the working dividend (0) by the divisor (8) to get the next digit in the solution of square root.

$$
\begin{array}{c|ccc}
 & 22 & {}_6 0 & {}_4 9 \\
 & & -56 & -49 \\
8 & & & 0 \\
\hline
 & 4 & 7 & 0 \\
\end{array}
$$

$$49 - 49 = 0 \text{ and } \frac{0}{8} = 0$$

Step 8.   As the initial problem (2209) is 4 digits, mark the decimal after 2 digits (4/2) from the left.

$$
\begin{array}{c|ccc}
 & 22 & {}_6 0 & {}_4 9 \\
 & & -56 & -49 \\
8 & & & 0 \\
\hline
 & 4 & 7 & .0 \\
\end{array}
$$

$$Therefore, \sqrt{2209} = 47$$

(2) Find the square root of 973.44

- Quick solution:

	9	7	$_1$3	$_0$4	$_0$4
		−6	−1	−4	−4
6			12	0	0
	3	1	.2	0	0

$$Therefore, \sqrt{97344} = 31.2$$

- Detailed steps:

Step 1.   For now ignore the decimal and work with the full problem (97344)

Step 2.   Calculate n. The number 97344 has odd number of digits (5 digits).

$$n = (Number\ of\ digits - 1)$$

Step 3.   The highest square below or equal to the working digit (9) is 9, therefore the highest square root is 3 (square root of 9). Write 3 as the first digit of square root.

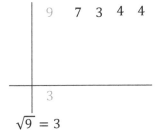

$$\sqrt{9} = 3$$

Step 4.   Multiply the SR (3) with 2 and write the product (6) as the divisor.

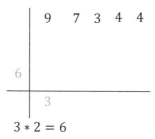

$$3 * 2 = 6$$

Step 5.   Divide the next gross dividend (7) by the divisor (6) and write the quotient below the gross dividend and the remainder as prefix to the next digit in the problem.

$$\frac{7}{6} \xrightarrow{\text{Results in}} 1 \text{ as the quotient and } 1 \text{ as the remainder}$$

Step 6.   Find the duplex of the quotient digits and write that below the next gross dividend. Exclude the first digit in the quotient while finding the duplex.

$$D(1) \xrightarrow{\text{Implies}} 1^2 = 1$$

Step 7.   Subtract the duplex (1) from the gross dividend (13) to get
the net dividend (12).

$$
\begin{array}{c|ccccc}
   & 9 & 7 & {}_1 3 & 4 & 4 \\
   &   & -6 & -1 &   &   \\
 6 &   &   & 12 &   &   \\
\hline
   & 3 & 1 &   &   &   \\
\end{array}
$$

Step 8.   Divide the net dividend (12) by the divisor (6) to get the
next quotient and the remainder. Prefix the remainder to the next
digit.

$$
\begin{array}{c|ccccc}
   & 9 & 7 & {}_1 3 & {}_0 4 & 4 \\
   &   & -6 & -1 &   &   \\
 6 &   &   & 12 &   &   \\
\hline
   & 3 & 1 & 2 &   &   \\
\end{array}
$$

$\dfrac{12}{6} \xrightarrow{\text{Results in}} 2$ *as the quotient and* 0 *as the remainder*

Step 9.   Find the duplex of the quotient excluding the first digit in
the quotient and write the duplex below the next gross dividend
(04).

$$
\begin{array}{c|ccccc}
   & 9 & 7 & {}_1 3 & {}_0 4 & 4 \\
   &   & -6 & -1 & -4 &   \\
 6 &   &   & 12 &   &   \\
\hline
   & 3 & 1 & 2 &   &   \\
\end{array}
$$

$D(12) \xrightarrow{\text{Implies}} 2 * 1 * 2 = 4$

Step 10.   Subtract the duplex (4) from the gross dividend (04) to get the net dividend (0). Divide this net dividend by the divisor to get the quotient (0) and the remainder (0) as prefix to the next digit in the problem.

$$
\begin{array}{c|ccccc}
 & 9 & 7 & {}_13 & {}_04 & {}_04 \\
 & & -6 & -1 & -4 & \\
6 & & & 12 & 0 & \\
\hline
 & 3 & 1 & 2 & 0 & \\
\end{array}
$$

$\dfrac{0}{6}$ *Results in* $\longrightarrow 0$ *as the quotient and 0 as the remainder*

Step 11.   Complete the final steps to get the complete quotient.

$$
\begin{array}{c|ccccc}
 & 9 & 7 & {}_13 & {}_04 & {}_04 \\
 & & -6 & -1 & -4 & -4 \\
6 & & & 12 & 0 & 0 \\
\hline
 & 3 & 1 & 2 & 0 & 0 \\
\end{array}
$$

$D(120) \xrightarrow{Implies} (2 * 1 * 0) + 2^2 = 4$

Step 12.   As the number of digits before the decimal in the initial problem were 3. Therefore place a decimal after $(3+1)/2 = 2$ digits from the left.

$$
\begin{array}{c|ccccc}
 & 9 & 7 & {}_13 & {}_04 & {}_04 \\
 & & -6 & -1 & -4 & -4 \\
6 & & & 12 & 0 & 0 \\
\hline
 & 3 & 1 & .2 & 0 & 0 \\
\end{array}
$$

$$Therefore, \sqrt{97344} = 31.2$$

Exercise 14 – Square root of any Number

1. 3249	2. 92743	3. 20540	4. 8543
5. 3610	6. 7744	7. 5184	8. 94620

Chapter 7.   CUBES OF TWO DIGIT NUMBERS

CUBES OF TWO DIGIT NUMBERS

Consider the cube formula $(ab)^3 = a^3 + 3a^2b + 3ab^2 + b^3$

The terms in the answer can be resolved into

1st term: $a^3 \xrightarrow{Resolves\ to} a^3$

2nd term: $3a^2b \xrightarrow{Resolves\ to}$

$3 * a^3 * \left(\frac{b}{a}\right) \xrightarrow{Resolves\ to} \left(a^3 * \left(\frac{b}{a}\right)\right) + \left(2 * a^3 * \left(\frac{b}{a}\right)\right)$

3rd term:

$3ab^2 \xrightarrow{Resolves\ to}$

$(a^2b) * \left(\frac{b}{a}\right) \xrightarrow{Resolves\ to} \left((a^2b) * \left(\frac{b}{a}\right)\right) + \left(2 * (a^2b) * \left(\frac{b}{a}\right)\right)$

4th term: $b^3 \xrightarrow{Resolves\ to} (ab^2) * \left(\frac{b}{a}\right)$

Therefore, $(ab)^3 =$

$(a^3) \quad \left(3 * a^3 * \left(\frac{b}{a}\right)\right) \quad \left(3 * a^3 * \left(\frac{b}{a}\right) * \left(\frac{b}{a}\right)\right)$

$\left(a^3 * \left(\frac{b}{a}\right) * \left(\frac{b}{a}\right) * \left(\frac{b}{a}\right)\right)$

(1) Find the cube of 46

- Quick solution: $(46)^3 =$

$(64) \quad \left(3 * 64 * \left(\frac{6}{4}\right)\right) \quad \left(3 * 64 * \left(\frac{6}{4}\right) * \left(\frac{6}{4}\right)\right)$

$$\left(64 * \left(\tfrac{6}{4}\right) * \left(\tfrac{6}{4}\right) * \left(\tfrac{6}{4}\right)\right)$$

$\xrightarrow{Implies} (64) \qquad (288) \qquad (432) \qquad (216)$

Therefore, $(46)^3 = 97336$

- Detailed steps: The number $(46)^3$ is of the form of $(ab)^3$

Step 1.   Find the terms in the answer

1.1. First term: $a^3 \xrightarrow{Implies} 4^3 = 64$

1.2. Second term: $3a^3 \left(\tfrac{b}{a}\right) \xrightarrow{Implies} 3 * 4^3 * \left(\tfrac{4}{6}\right) = 288$

1.3. Third term: $3a^3 \left(\tfrac{b}{a}\right)\left(\tfrac{b}{a}\right) \xrightarrow{Implies}$

$$3 * 4^3 * \left(\tfrac{4}{6}\right) * \left(\tfrac{4}{6}\right) = 432$$

1.4. Fourth term: $a^3 \left(\tfrac{b}{a}\right)\left(\tfrac{b}{a}\right)\left(\tfrac{b}{a}\right) \xrightarrow{Implies}$

$$4^3 * \left(\tfrac{4}{6}\right) * \left(\tfrac{4}{6}\right) * \left(\tfrac{4}{6}\right) = 216$$

Step 2.   Retain one digit at each position in the answer and carry-forward the rest of the digits

$\xrightarrow{Implies} (64)(288)(432 + 21)(6)$

$\xrightarrow{Implies} (64)(288)(432 + 21)(6)$

$\xrightarrow{Implies} (64)(288 + 45)(3)(6)$

$\xrightarrow{Implies} (64 + 33)(3)(3)(6)$

$\xrightarrow{Implies} (97)(3)(3)(6)$

Therefore, $(46)^3 = 97336$

Exercise 15 – Cubes of Two Digit Numbers

1. **72**	2. **857**	3. **403**	4. **220**
5. **371**	6. 89	7. 1110	8. 24

Chapter 8.   APPLICATION OF SPEED MATH

(1) A fruit seller had some apples. He sells 37% apples and still has 441 apples. How many apples did the fruit seller originally have?

Solution: $x - \frac{37x}{100} = 441 \xrightarrow{Implies} x - 0.37x = 441 \xrightarrow{Implies} x = \frac{44100}{63}$

$\xrightarrow[\quad by\ flag \quad]{Performing\ division} x = 700\ apples$

(2) The ratio between the perimeter and the breadth of a rectangle is $5:1$. If the area of the rectangle is $216\ cm^2$, what is the length of the rectangle?

Solution: $\frac{(2l+2b)}{b} = \frac{5}{1} \xrightarrow{Implies} b = \frac{2l}{3}$

Also, $l * b = 216 \xrightarrow{Implies} l * \frac{2l}{3} = 216 \xrightarrow{Implies} l^2 = 216 * \frac{3}{2}$

Therefore, $l = \sqrt{324}$

$\xrightarrow[\quad]{Using\ the\ square\ root\ technique} l = 18\ cms$

(3) As shown on a travel map, one route measures $6\frac{1}{2}$ inches and the other $24\frac{1}{2}$ inches. If 1 inch represents 22 miles, what is the difference in miles between the two routes?

Solution:

$6\frac{1}{2}\ in = \frac{13}{2}\ in \xrightarrow{Implies} 22 * \frac{13}{2}\ miles =$

$$11 * 13 \; miles \xrightarrow[\text{with 11}]{\text{Multiplication}} 413 \; miles$$

$$24\frac{1}{2} \; in = \frac{49}{2} \; in \xrightarrow{\text{Implies}} 22 * \frac{49}{2} \; miles =$$

$$11 * 49 \; miles \xrightarrow[\text{with 11}]{\text{Multiplication}} 539 \; miles$$

Therefore, the difference is $539 - 413 = 126 \; miles$

(4) After collecting the parcel a delivery boy leaves the office and drives at a speed of 45 kms/hr. The next delivery boy leaves 99 minutes later to deliver a high priority parcel and travels at 60 kms/hr speed. How far would the first delivery boy have travelled before being overtaken by the second delivery boy? Solution:

Distance travelled by first delivery boy = distance travelled by the second delivery boy

$$45\frac{kms}{hr} = 0.75\frac{km}{min} \; and \; 60\frac{kms}{hr} = 1\frac{km}{min}$$

Therefore, $0.75 * (t + 99) = 1 * t \xrightarrow{\text{Implies}}$

$$0.75 * 99 = 0.25t \xrightarrow[\text{with 9s imply}]{\text{Multiplication}} 74.25 = 0.25t$$

Therefore, the second delivery boy will overtake the first delivery boy at 297 minutes.

(5) A packing unit has to pack 6408 apples in boxes such that each box should contain equal number of apples. If the maximum number of available boxes is 90 how many boxes will be required to pack all the apples and how many apples will be packed in each box?

Solution: To find apples per bag perform$\frac{6408}{90}$. As 6408 is not fully divisible by 90 perform

*Applying division
by*
$$\frac{6408}{89} \xrightarrow{\textit{divisor less than base}}$$

72 apples per box and 89 boxes will be required

(6) A dishonest shopkeeper professes to selling pulses at the cost price, but he uses a false weight of 890gms per kg. What will be his % gain if he sells 890 grams of pulses and gains 110 grams?

Solution: If he sells 100 grams of pulses then he will gain (110 / 890) *100 = 12.4%

(7) A Software Engineer has the capability of thinking 100 lines of code in five minutes and can type 100 lines of code in 10 minutes. He takes a break for five minutes after every ten minutes. How many lines of codes will he complete typing after an hour?

Solution: Break after every 15 min, therefore 4 breaks in 1 hr = 20 min break in 1 hr, working mins is 40 min, codes written will be 100/15*40 = 20/3*40 =6.7*40= 250 app

(8) A man was engaged on a job for 30 days on the condition that he would get a wage of Rs. 10 for the day he works, but he has to pay a fine of Rs. 2 for each day of his absence. For how many days was he absent from work if he gets Rs. 216 at the end of 30 days?

Solution: For every day he loses 10+2 = 12 rs, therefore 300- 216=84/12 is his absence

(9) In a certain store, the profit is 320% of the cost. If the cost increases by 25% but the selling price remains constant, approximately what

percentage of the selling price is the profit?

Solution: Consider the Cost Price = Rs. 100

Therefore, $Selling\ price = 100 + 320 = 420$

$New\ cost\ price = 100 + 25 = 125$, New selling price = 420,

$New\ profit = 420 - 125 = 295$

$$New\ profit\ percentage = \frac{295}{420} * 100\%$$

$$= \frac{1475}{21}\% \xrightarrow{Flag\ division} 70\%$$

(10)   A car driving at the speed of 20 km/hr crosses a pole in 3 seconds. What is the length of the car?

Solutions:

$$Speed = 20kmph = 20 * \frac{5}{18}mps = \frac{50}{9}mps \xrightarrow[\text{by 9 technique}]{Division} 5.56\ mps$$

Length of the car = $Speed * time = 5.56 * 3 = 16.68\ mts$

Answers

Answers 1 – Find the Complement of

1. **52652**	2. **63410**	3. **6443**	4. **7930**
5. **1011**	6. 10	7. 89000	8. 7252

Answers 2 – Solve mental multiplication with 9s problems

1. **27729**	2. **774774**	3. **8694297**	4. **83921607**
5. **57764223**	6. 537471	7. 654417	8. 601029
9. **5570424**	10. 15921	11. 81257661	12. 89216694
13. **599940**	14. 62469	15. 4387608	16. 44343

Answers 3 – Solve multiplication with 1s problems

1. 498223	2. 6335325	3. 881166	4. 8712
5. 10505484	6. 6130498	7. 535502	8. 7428146
9. 54477233	10. 997678	11. 4522881	12. 48884
13. 6187029	14. 438845	15. 5899641	16. 57772

Answers 4 – Solve multiplication with multiples of 11 problems

1. **91272**	2. **1270122**	3. **946010**	4. **448812**
5. **23814**	6. 82032	7. 126546	8. 109772
9. **6539**	10. 126720	11. 66072	12. 39116

Answers 5 – Solve multiplication with numbers close to bases

1. **8265**	2. **7719**	3. **7470**	4. **8240**
5. **9010**	6. 9523	7. 9579	8. 9870
9. **51294**	10. 93436	11. 10710	12. 10506

Answers 6 – Solve any number multiplication problems

1. **595584**	2. **165850**	3. **420021**	4. **395827**
5. **916749**	6. 916749	7. 8280	8. 7682
9. **3169928**	10. 4812780	11. 2639146	12. 4278261

Answers 7 – Perform subtraction

1. **2629**	2. **4514**	3. **742**	4. **2829**
5. **3966**	6. 1840	7. 25104	8. 43809

Answers 8 – Quick division by 9

1. **Q6909, R3**	2. **Q1094, R6**	3. **Q9569, R0**	4. **Q1821, R3**
5. **Q6814, R5**	6. Q4403, R0	7. Q7970, R8	8. Q11091, R1
9. **Q9618, R1**	10. Q8294, R2	11. Q4150, R4	12. Q8362, R5
13. **Q2029, R0**	14. Q10920, R0	15. Q3984, R1	16. Q7796, R4

Answers 9 – Quick Division with Divisor close to its Base

1. **Q622, R10**	2. **Q1077, R43**	3. **Q595, R6**	4. **Q547, R93**
5. **Q861, R61**	6. Q453, R11	7. Q361, R72	8. Q354, R47

Answers 10 – Any Number division using flagged divisor

1. **38.495**	2. **33.619**	3. **130.6774**	4. **369.9506**
5. **81.994**	6. 313.7784	7. 9.01495	8. 284.6293
9. **110.9814**	10. 144.1885	11. 214.0212	12. 8.96362

Answers 11 – Checking for Errors

1. **Correct**	2. **Incorrect**	3. **Incorrect**	4. **Correct**
5. **Incorrect**	6. Correct	7. Incorrect	8. Correct

Answers 12 – Working with Fractions

1. **0.12195**	2. **0.210526**	3. **0.33333**	4. **0.8235294**
5. **0.44444**	6. 0.9642857	7. 0.5263158	8. 0.0555556
9. **0.10526315**	10. 0.6363636	11. 0.736842105	12. 0.089743589

Answers 13 – Squares of any Numbers

1. **4225**	2. **55225**	3. **7225**	4. **329476**
5. **93045316**	6. 17842176	7. 81144064	8. 58369600

Answers 14 – Square root of any Number

1. **57**	2. **304.5374**	3. **143.3178**	4. **92.4284**
5. **996.7999**	6. 88	7. 72	8. 307.6036

Answers 15 – Cubes of Two Digit Numbers

1. **373248**	2. **629422793**	3. **65450827**	4. **10648000**
5. **51064811**	6. 704969	7. 1331000	8. 13824

Contact details

You may order your copy of book online through amazon.com, createspace.com, lulu.com, pothi.com

Send your feedback to apasha016@gmail.com

Join me on twitter apasha016

CPSIA information can be obtained at www.ICGtesting.com
Printed in the USA
LVOW04s2142180914

404758LV00029B/1316/P

9 781492 393986